The Calling of the Laity

Verna Dozier's Anthology

An Alban Institute Publication

The Publications Program of The Alban Institute is assisted by a grant from Trinity Church, New York City.

Library of Congress Catalog Card #88-070761.

CONTENTS

ACKNOWLEDGMENTS

The following articles: "Ministry in the Marketplace," by William E. Diehl; "Ministries Outside the Parish," by Mark Gibbs; "Faith and Politics: Our Ministry as Citizens," by Eleanor N. Lewis and Mimi Waxter; and "Prophets to Profit," by Robert K. Massie, Jr. are reprinted by permission of *Ministry Development Journal*, The Episcopal Church Center, 815 Second Avenue, New York, NY 10017.

"Saturday's Ministries," by Mark Gibbs is reprinted from *Gifts*, Summer/Fall, 1986, copyright 1982, by permission of Audenshaw Foundation, 2 Eaton Gate, London SW1 W-9BL, England.

"Hazardous Waste and Holy Ground," by John Finn is printed from *Centering*, Volume III, No. 2, Spring 1986 with permission of the author.

"Confronting the National Security State," an interview with Margie and John Gilbert by Mary Lou Suhor with Robert L. DeWitt is excerpted from *The Witness*, April 1987. "Is This Ministry?" by Nell Braxton Gibson is from *The Witness*, Vol. 64, No. 9, Sept. 1981. They are reprinted with permission of the publisher.

"Service Is Her Business," by Bill Robinson is reprinted with permission from *The Berea Alumnus*, July-August 1987.

"The Ministry of the Laity, Reflections for Study and Debate," by Neil M. Alexander is reprinted from *Links*, Winter 1985, with permission of General Board of Discipleship, The United Methodist Church, Nashville, TN.

Excerpts from "Challenge to Ministry: Opportunities for Older Persons," by Emma Lou Benignus are reprinted with permission of the Episcopal Society for Ministry on Aging, Inc. from the book, *Affirmative Aging: A Resource for Ministry*, Harper & Row, 1985, U.S.A.

Where are the ministers of the laity?

Over a year ago the Alban Institute sent out this call:

> The Alban Institute would like to publish an anthology of articles on the ministry of the laity and would appreciate selections and suggestions for possible pieces to be included.

> The anthology will be directed to experiences, issues, problems, "think pieces" about carrying out into the world of work (*especially*) and into the community (local, national and international) ministry that is entrusted to us.

> Questions that might be addressed are: (1) "How does one make decisions when the choice is only between lesser evils?" (2) "How does one live with the incomplete—never quite making it, when all around the hucksters are proclaiming easy answers?" (3) "How can we educate so that the resources of the faith are there for strength and not solutions?"

This anthology contains twice as many articles in the third category as in the other two.

That points up a problem. Loren Mead, director of the Institute, has said that even with all the talk about the ministry of the laity, nothing really seems to have happened.

It may be we are looking in the wrong place. We are looking to the institutional church. To use Celia Hahn's phrase, the church is acting like "a world in itself." To use Pat Drake's phrase, "the laity are being shortchanged." Their world is not considered important.

To find out about laity, *go where they are*—where they are working, struggling, trying, failing, picking themselves up, and carrying on. The church as institution needs to attend to those places.

The church is the "in-order-that" institution, the institution in order that ministry may happen in the world.

Bruce Reed wrote ten years ago in an Alban Institute publication, *The* Task of the Church and the Role of its Members:

> ... the purpose of the church is to prepare these members so that the profane world—(the world outside the temple)—can take on the qualities of the Kingdom.
>
> This is brought about as those who are its members are given the capacity to 'see' the Kingdom; that is, to accept that the qualities of the Kingdom—justice, peace, righteousness, and freedom—are the normative relationship. ...

For the institutional church to have any idea of how well it is doing, it must know what its members are doing in the world.

This anthology contains a sermon by an editor who recounts graphically an ethical struggle. His priest knew about that struggle. Another pastor commented on the theological statement a parish made by literally making its building a window on the world. And a third member of the clergy used his sabbatical time to study at the Harvard Business School.

The institutional church needs to pay more attention to where the laity works out its salvation—and the transformation of the world. Professional magazines, syndicated columnists, biographies, works of fiction—these are all places where sensitive and astute ordained ministers and professional church workers can find out what the laity are doing and where the institutional church needs to be engaged.

PART I

Making Decisions

The work of the lay person is making decisions—juggling one possibility against another. Not the good against the bad, (that is easy to do; fanatics have no problem) but deciding in favor of the less bad and against what is perceived as the more bad.

Politics is the great arena for decision making. Eleanor N. Lewis and Mimi Waxter, who feel strongly the call to live out the "so what" of the Christian faith, report on an educational venture in "Faith and Politics: Our Ministry as Citizens."

Politics is the grist for the mill of the newspaper editor, and sometimes he or she is faced with an agonizing decision about what to print. Chris Satullo, managing editor for news at his local paper, had to make such a decision, and his priest, The Rev. James L. Gill of Trinity Episcopal Church, Easton, Pennsylvania, asked him to preach about it as part of the parish's regular offering of lay sermons on matters of faith and everyday life.

The story of Jewrette Johnson, a graduate of Berea College, was reported in the college journal. Ms. Johnson lives out the values of the Kingdom without any recourse to "religious language" and attributes her sense of justice and her courage to the influence of a teacher.

Robert K. Massie, Jr., encountered the financial world at a more exalted level. He acknowledges that he had stood outside the corporate club for years and criticized it. Then he decided to find out what business was all about. What were the issues struggled with? What were the choices made—and why?

I have included two articles on the ministry of the laity by Neil M. Alexander of the General Board of Discipleship of the United Methodist Church—the first on the importance of paying attention to our communities and the world, and the second on the vocation all of us have as servants of the living Christ.

No anthology on the ministry of the laity would be complete without an article by Mark Gibbs. In this article the dean of the lay ministry movement tackles the all-important issue of making decisions about the use of leisure time.

Faith and Politics:
Our Ministry as Citizens

by Eleanor N. Lewis and Mimi Waxter

Who should be involved in politics? A program on citizenship as ministry (described here), was led by two parishioners—one with experience in politics and citizen education, and the other with a special interest in theology and lay ministry.

On most Sundays during the fall, winter and spring at the Church of the Redeemer in Baltimore, there is a one-hour Forum before the 10:30 service on subjects of Christian concern. These are planned by the Adult Education and Critical Issues committees, and forum leaders are from within as well as outside the parish. Subjects have varied from medical ethics to nuclear arms to meditations on the lectionary. Attendance may fluctuate from less than 10 to over 30.

By 9:15 we had arranged on walls and tables maps of election districts, leaflets on how to address representatives, registration forms, and the booklet "Policy for Action" listing General Convention's positions on public issues. These materials had been assembled with the assistance of the City Board of Elections, city and county Leagues of Women Voters, and the Public Policy Network at the Episcopal Church Center, all of whom had been extremely interested and helpful.

After greetings and introductions, we began.

"We've talked recently about two kinds of ministry: first, our ministry to each other *in* the church, where we get the nourishment and the support we need for our ministry in the world. The other is what we might call direct ministry to people beyond these walls—family, friends and neighbors, those we serve in our daily work, poor and hungry people, lonely people, people in trouble. This includes volunteer work in social agencies, and parish programs.

"Another ministry to which all of us are called is our role as citizens of a democracy. This is not much emphasized in most parishes, for understandable reasons of history and tradition. The center of our life together, for many people their *only* experience of parish life, is our worship in church on Sundays and other special occasions. This is based on the Prayer Book, and the Prayer Book is based on the Bible, often word for word. We are a *Bible* church.

"The Bible has quite a lot to say about God's will for the king. The government was on *his* shoulders, then and for many centuries to come. The point I'd like to make is that in a democratic country we, its citizens, *are* the king. The ultimate authority under God is not in the hands of mayors or governors or representatives or courts or even the President. It is in ours. We are the rulers, and if we neglect our role as citizens, or act out of carelessness or prejudice or mere self-interest, we are bad rulers. We are the ones who need to listen when God says to the King, 'Execute justice in the morning, and deliver from the hand of the oppressor him who has been robbed, lest my wrath go forth like fire and burn with none to quench it, because of your evil doings.'

"Let's hear a few more examples of God's word to kings, thinking how we might apply them to ourselves. Solomon, newly annointed king, prayed for help: 'I am but a little child; I do not know how to go out or come in.' Haven't we all felt like that? He asked to be given an understanding mind, and his prayer was answered. The Psalms stress the king's dependence on God: 'A king is not saved by his great army.' 'In thy strength the king rejoices, O Lord.' In Proverbs: 'The king's heart is a stream of water in the hand of the Lord; he turns it wherever he will.' In Ecclesiastics: 'Better is a poor and wise youth than an old and foolish king.' And in Jeremiah: 'Go down to the—King of Judah and say, "Thus says the Lord. Do justice and righteousness.—Do no wrong or violence to the alien, the fatherless and the widow, nor shed innocent blood in this place!"

"Our prayer for the President comes from the English prayer for the king, as suggested in Paul's letter to Timothy: 'Pray for kings and all who are in authority.' This, of course, was rewritten for our church when we became a separate nation; but we still pray for the President as if he were king, forgetting that God may be calling us to *write* to the President also, whether in support, criticism, or suggestions for future action. In God's eyes he too is 'but a little child,' and we have a ministry in him and through him, and through 'all in authority' to our country.

"In the Book of Common Prayer there are *many* prayers for those in authority—in collects, litanies, Prayers of the People at the Eucharist. In a Prayer for Peace we ask God to guide 'those who take counsel for the nations of the earth,' but there is no suggestion

that with God's help *we* might give them some guidance. Nevertheless, in several places it *is* suggested that we ourselves have something to do about things like justice, peace, and poverty, as in the
First Litany for Morning Prayer: 'Guide us in the way of Justice and
Peace, Let not the needy be forgotten.' The Prayer for Social Justice
surely *suggests* our vocation as citizens: 'Grant us grace fearlessly to
contend against evil and to make no peace with oppression,' and
'help us to employ (our freedom) in the maintenance of justice in
our communities and among the nations.' The wonderful, familiar
Prayer for Guidance is as helpful in our *political* decisions as in any
others we have to make.

"Finally, on page 822, under prayers 'For Sound Government,' I
found what I was looking for. After prayers for the President, the
Cabinet, Governors, Mayors, Senators and Representatives, Legisla-
tors, Judges and Officers of the Court, we pray:

> And finally, teach our people to rely on your strength and to
> accept their responsibilities to their fellow citizens, that they
> may elect trustworthy leaders and make wise decisions for the
> well being of our society.

"Another thing that has changed, in scope though not in principle,
is the answer to the question, Who is my neighbor? Jesus' answer
still holds because he didn't say, 'Your fellow Jew,' as earlier inter-
preters might have maintained. Instead, he told a story that turned
the question around and made 'neighbor' mean one who helps,
regardless of race or religion or nationality. 'My neighbor' has been
defined as 'anyone it is in my power to befriend.' What has changed
is that by our actions, or our failure to act, and especially through
our government, we are now able to help, or hurt, people all over
the world.

"The great English Archbishop William Temple said in one of
his books that to be a true Christian you have to be a politician.
Remembering that each of us has to do this in his or her own way,
I think he was right!"

Then we asked some questions: "How many of you have ever
visited the city jail? The Department of Social Services? Attended a
meeting of the City or County Council?"

We distributed copies of a questionnaire on "The City," and after
completing them, compared our answers against the facts. This
activity was illuminating to most of us and sparked a good deal of
discussion, from which we established the following steps. We are
called to our communities as Christians and citizens. Not all of us

will, or can, do all of these things, but it is important to know that they are as much a part of Christian ministry as serving on a parish committee, visiting a sick neighbor, or working in a soup kitchen.

First, *be informed*

On problems within your community and government agencies concerned with them. For many of us, this means visiting institutions, neighborhoods, people we would ordinarily never see.

On social and political issues.

On the duties and powers of elected officials.

On candidates for elective office.

Second, *take action*

By personal involvement in the community, including service on boards and commissions. By voting for your chosen candidates.

By working for and/or giving to candidates of your choice.

By writing, telephoning or visiting elected officials. (They want, and need, to hear from us.)

By writing letters to newspapers.

By testifying at public hearings.

A real help, for both learning and action, is to join an organization concerned with government, such as the non-partisan League of Women Voters, political clubs, and groups working on a single issue such as environment or peace. It's good to talk about issues and candidates, and listen to other people's opinions even, perhaps especially, when you disagree. It is necessary, and our faith will help us stand up in the face of controversy. Members of a parish, friends and neighbors, husbands and wives disagree without ceasing to love and respect each other.

Because some politicians are self-serving or dishonest or both, many good people think it's wrong to "get mixed up in politics." When honest people feel this way, the undesirable leaders flourish. This ministry is too important to be left to them!

After the discussion several participants suggested this material should be shared with more people. The following Sunday we set up a table at the coffee hour with our maps, leaflets and mimeographed papers. Parishioners took many of the materials, studied the district map, and asked questions. We found the whole program worthwhile, and hope to build on it in the future.

Eleanor N. Lewis is a member of the Peace and Justice Commission of the Diocese of Maryland. She was one of the first chairpersons of the Executive Council's Program Group on Lay Ministry, serving from 1970 to 1972.

Mimi Waxter is a life-long member of the Church of the Redeemer and is the coordinator of a loan fund for housing that benefits low income families in the Baltimore area.

Lay Ministry Battle Story: Grey Areas in Black Type

by Chris Satullo

Chris Satullo, Express *managing editor, preached this sermon at Trinity Church, Easton, Pennsylvania.*

As some of you may know, I work as an editor at *The Express*. Editor is one of those jobs everyone has heard of, but few can really fathom. What do editors do, anyway, besides be colorful, grouse about dangling participles and swear a lot?

One of the editor's functions is to be a gatekeeper. He's the one who insists things belong in the paper despite the resistance of some people. He's also the one who resists putting things in the paper, despite the insistence of other people.

Is such work a ministry? Is it in any way even tangential to the Gospel? I truly believe so, but sometimes I have a funny way of showing it.

Let me tell you two stories about me as editor and gatekeeper. At first glance, they might seem to paint me as a hypocrite, or at least mightily confused.

At a second glance, I hope they will seem emblematic of the struggle we all face to resolve the tension between faith in Jesus Christ and the civil religion of the work place.

I write a column for *The Express*. Recently I wrote with some emotion in that column about how a newspaper should act with a sense of brotherhood, a special bond of caring, toward its readers.

The day after the column ran, a phone rang in the newsroom. It was a reader with a tale too sad to be untrue. Her husband had died a year ago, she said, tragically young. Shortly after his death, she discovered she was with child. Widowed, unable to work while taking care of a baby and another small child, she had fallen behind on the bills; now, the only way out was a bankruptcy petition. What she wanted from us, what she pleaded for, was for us not to publish any mention of her bankruptcy case.

I had to tell her I was sorry, but if bankruptcy court in Reading sent us notice of her petition, as they have countless others, we would publish it, as we have countless others, briefly, with no fanfare, but nonetheless in irrevocable black and white.

Nice guy, huh?

Now, let me wind the clock back a few more weeks to a day you probably all remember, a Thursday when the world turned white in our annual blizzard. Again, my column was caught in a contradiction.

That day I carried on at length in the column about the existence of a commercial videotape called "Faces of Death," a vile exercise in which various snippets of film of real people suffering real death have been stitched together for the amusement of the perverse. Like it or not, this tape is a big mover in video stores. I don't like it and said so in sharp language in the column.

I also happened to be in charge of the front page that day. We were attempting to wrap up the paper early because of the snow, to give our drivers more time to battle the drifts. At 11 a.m., I was holding a spot for one more story. Pennsylvania's state treasurer, Budd Dwyer, was scheduled to resign his office that morning because of a bribery conviction.

Of course you all know what Budd Dwyer did that day. We found out at about 11:20, a scant 10 minutes before my deadline. The first story did not move over the Associated Press wire for about 10 minutes, and after deadline we were still waiting for a photo.

Though my first reaction to the news was a feeling of sickened shock, it was quickly supplanted by a sense of intensity and yes, excitement. Moments like this, when a big story breaks at deadline, fully test the craft of the journalist. Any journalist who tells you he doesn't relish those moments, no matter how awful the event that produces them, is a liar.

I tore apart the existing front page, redesigned it to make Dwyer's public suicide the dominant story and went back to pray over our wirephoto machine. About 11:45, with time evaporating for us, the first photo moved.

It was the awful photo of Dwyer with gun in mouth that ran in our paper that day. With the publisher and managing editor hovering over my shoulder, I made the split-second determination that, as horrible as it was, the photo should be used, given the significance of the news. After that split second of moral calculus, my energies were devoted solely to getting that photo onto the page and that page onto the press. That was my job—to put a face of death on page A-1, while deploring them on page A-4.

To any journalist, those two split-second, but echoing decisions—to reject a troubled woman, to accept a troubling photo—can be reconciled rather easily with the canons of the craft. If you publish it consistently, without regard to the social status of the subject. Besides, in newsrooms, we've all learned that the fraudulent are as adept at telling sob stories as the truly injured.

Dwyer's suicide was a major news event. Most newspeople would agree that their job was to report it prominently, in a way that conveyed, rather than ignored, how shocking and awful it was.

But, in this sanctuary, the canons of journalism are weightless.

All that matters is the word of God.

Can the demands of craft be reconciled to the demands of the Gospel? For those of us rooted in the secular, but yearning to believe that the secular offers room for ministry, for holiness and grace, no question is more compelling.

As a newcomer to Trinity Church, I have been struck by how hard this congregation works to make the connection between faith and daily life, between what people do Sunday in church and what they do the rest of the week. That quest makes faith more fulfilling, but also more dangerous, because it can no longer be safely compartmentalized. Trinity teaches that witness is not just a weekend hobby; it is just as important around the office water cooler as at the communion rail.

Just as important—but harder. In the work place, there is more ambiguity, more distraction. There are more false gods, false values, more temptations to be like the Pharisees of today's Gospel (Jn. 91-13, 28-38).

When I think about that Gospel, I have to confess how very like the Pharisees I sometimes am in my work as an editor.

The Pharisees are men of rules, who seek to tame the frightful moral and emotional ambiguity of living by reducing holiness, morality to a set of formal policies. They like things neat. A right way, a wrong way. A villain, and a hero (usually themselves). No painful mysteries that prove to be occasions of grace.

If, for example, a blind man (or a woman in bankruptcy) came to them in need, they would offer him not help, but rules. "Sorry, fella, no healing on the Sabbath" or "Sorry, it's against our policy."

The Pharisees also are, like any good reporter, professional skeptics. When an event occurs that rattles their world view, such as a blind man gaining sight on the Sabbath, they suspect fraud and seek to sniff it out with a worthy investigative zeal. They are ruthless in discounting the testimony of a man they consider to be an unreliable source—a mere blind beggar.

The irony of this Gospel, of course, is that it is these Pharisees who are blind, while the blind man sees Jesus clearly, and proclaims him Lord.

What blinds the Pharisees is their faith in their own righteousness and wisdom, in their limited world view.

The work places of America are full of Pharisees, people, often well-meaning, whose vision of the Gospel is obstructed by their loyalty to the religion of their craft, their work.

Make no mistake—the work place is this nation's great, unrecognized church; each work place, each profession has its own culture, its own set of values. They are largely unexamined, but they are relentlessly inculcated, relentlessly enforced. For many, this religion is more persuasive, more powerful than anything they observe on Sunday. It can become a false God we place before the real one. Newspapers certainly have a strong work culture, a credo that places high value on skepticism, tough-mindedness and rigorous truthfulness. Those values can easily slide into something less appetizing—callousness and cynicism.

Some rotten people work at newspapers, and do very well in the eyes of the world. And, sometimes, to do well in the eyes of my workplace, I do rotten things, like running photos on the front page that many people find offensive. My civil religion can be at war with the Gospel.

Is the conflict hopeless? Are the canons of my craft nothing more than a false God that pulls me away from the Gospel?

I don't think so, or I wouldn't be in the business or love it so. No matter how often my work seems to others, or to myself, to be a grubby enterprise, to be a matter of harping, indeed, feasting, upon the misfortune of others, I still see in it an opportunity for Christian witness.

The readings today buttress the hope that the potential for holiness can reside in what seems utterly humble, hopelessly mundane.

In the book of Samuel, the youngest son of Jesse, the one everyone overlooked because he was assigned the scut work of tending the sheep, proves to be God's anointed. In the Gospel, a blind beggar is the only person capable of recognizing and proclaiming the Good News.

Scripture reminds us constantly that, as God's people, we are called to a holiness that emulates His holiness. But this holiness does not amount to an austere withdrawal from the world. That is the easy way out.

To heal a blind man, Jesus didn't raise his eyes aloft and whisper a prayer. He spat on the ground and then got his hands dirty making clay.

In the same way, we are to risk venturing into a fallen, broken world, getting its muck all over our hands, but somehow turning that muck into gold.

We must, in other words, make our work our witness, our ministry. To do that, we must judge the canons of our craft, our workplace religion, in the light of the Gospel; in that light, they will either be redeemed, or revealed as false Gods.

I do see redeeming value in my work.

There is a passage in Leviticus that says to the people of God: "You shall do no injustice in judgment; you shall not be partial to the poor or defer to the great, but in righteousness shall you judge your neighbor. You shall not go up and down as a slanderer among your people."

When I read those words, I see a pretty fair description of a good journalist. That makes me feel pretty good about what I do. Besides toughness and cynicism, the credo of news work also includes a thirst for social justice, a sympathy for the wounded and downtrodden, a willingness to resist the abuse of power, a delight in celebrating good news.

But, still, but still. . .the Lord catches us in our craftiness.

He reminds us, with a phone call from a desperate woman, with the destructive act of a desperate man, that the fit of faith and craft are not always perfect. We assume that they are at the peril of our souls.

Our work culture and Jesus' clarion call to a difficult holiness do collide—frequently in some professions, occasionally in all.

It is hard to know what to do at these moments of collision. It is hard even to recognize them for what they are. So rarely is the equation clearcut—this way the Gospel, that way the blindness of human wisdom—and you have so little time to weigh the moral calculus. Sometimes, as the snowflakes fall and deadline approaches, you have only seconds.

It is a huge daily struggle, but it is the struggle we are called upon to undertake. Each day we must examine the religion of our work place and nudge it a little closer toward the Gospel, at least in the way we work, if not in the way our colleagues do.

This struggle is more than we, in our worldly wisdom, can manage by ourselves. We require, first of all, the grace of God, and secondly, the help and support of a community of faith.

Without those, as we go to work each day, we are simply wanderers in a confused and broken land.

With them, we can be people on the mission of the Gospel.

Let us pray for God's grace, and let us, by all means, help one another.

Service Is Her Business

by Bill Robinson

When Jewrette Johnson, '77, went to work for First Alabama Bank in Birmingham, she had one apprehension. "Will I be able to help people in this job?" she wondered.

"I found out right away," she says, "that the answer was *yes!*"

Service, the principle preached so often at Berea, is also the key to success in business, she says.

Whether it was helping a customer balance an account, solve a problem, complete a successful loan application or find the savings plan with the highest rate of return, Johnson found that personal service was what customers appreciated. "Even if a customer had only a nominal savings account, I gave them personal attention and saw that they got the best rate of return the bank offered," says Johnson, known to her friends as J.J. "I wanted all my customers to say, 'She's my banker'."

Her first assignments were in neighborhood branch offices, and "I really enjoyed the work there," she recalls. "Most branch customers have only small accounts, but helping them always gave me a good feeling. Because their accounts were small, even the little things you did were very important to them."

Johnson's reward for taking such care with small accounts turned out to be more than simply a good feeling. Today she is a financial services officer in the bank's central office serving "up-scale" customers.

In financial services, Johnson assists customers with investing their funds, a job that has grown more challenging as interest rates have fallen. "When I started, this job was easier, because rates of return on certificates of deposit and treasury bills were so high. Now with lower rates, finding the instrument that best suits an individual's needs is much tougher."

Johnson's attention to customer needs has built her a reputation that has helped draw new customers to the bank. Customer development is a big part of her job, and she calls on eight to ten prospects each day. Her efforts last year brought 237 new accounts to the bank, providing it with $11 million in new business.

"At times, I try not to smile so much," she says, afraid that she may not be displaying a banker's serious demeanor. "But I really enjoy my work and meeting people."

The management training program at First Alabama gives young bankers a thorough orientation in all phases of the business. One exercise Johnson remembers well was helping a customer open a checking account. "This was important to me," she confesses, "because I never had a checking account, and I could identify with the examples the instructors gave. I was glad we had that training, because I then knew how to have access to my money when the bank automatically deposited a salary check into my account that week."

This experience led Johnson to be enthusiastic about the bank's program to teach money management to public school students. "We teach students the basics of managing a savings or checking account," she explains. "They get a practice check book so they can learn to be more responsible with their money." And when they are ready to open an account, the young people may remember which bank cared enough to teach them about checking.

Another episode in her training stands out in Johnson's memory. After her orientation in the credit and installment loan departments, she was asked to analyze a credit review done by a senior officer.

What was supposed to be a "calm situation" turned out to be "more complicated than it appeared on the surface."

The trainee found that the senior officer did not strictly conform to bank guidelines for extending credit. "He was a branch manager, and here I was, a new employee. How dare I tell him that he was not following bank policy," she recalls. I didn't want to offend anyone, but on the other hand, I wanted to do the job right."

When she appeared before a credit review committee, the bank's loan director and personnel director were both present. "It was enough to make you a little nervous," she remembers. "But they complimented me on giving a 'comprehensive' review."

While many of her colleagues thought it was unfair for her to have such a difficult first assignment, she says she doesn't believe it was done deliberately. "In any case, it worked to my advantage," she says.

After the meeting, Johnson was told she was "going downtown" to a loan desk to review credit applications.

One of her first experiences in speaking up for what she thought was right, the bank executive says, came in an Issues and

Values class at Berea taught by Dr. Carl Kilbourne, '43. "I grew up in an environment where young people did not question their elders," she points out. "But in Dr. Kilbourne's class, everybody had a voice and your opinion was considered."

Kilbourne also encouraged his students to reach for their greatest potential, she recalls. "I was limiting myself, and I think he could see that. He made me believe I could do anything I wanted to do." That experience taught her that "there was more to learning than academics."

Her academic training has been important to her banking career, she adds. "Berea's curriculum broadens the horizon of its students. My studies in the liberal arts have helped me understand and communicate with people of many different backgrounds. In business, you need to know more than just dollars and cents."

Prophets to Profit

by Robert K. Massie, Jr.

The first time I walked around the Harvard Graduate School of Business Administration and looked at its massive and elegant buildings, its manicured lawns and pampered flora, I thought of Moses. According to the third chapter of the book of Exodus, as Moses stood on Mount Sinai before the burning bush he heard a voice that said, "Come no nearer, take off your shoes; the place you are standing on is holy ground."

As we went around the room introducing ourselves in class, I counted 2 lawyers, 8 consultants, 9 accountants, 17 engineers and 23 bankers. Twenty-five of my classmates had gone to Ivy League schools and 35 had majored in economics or business administration. Of those who had worked for large corporations before business school, four had worked for oil companies, three had worked for Procter & Gamble, three had worked for IBM, and two were currently on leave from General Motors. One fellow had been a captain in the Cold Stream Guards and had led a platoon in Northern Ireland; another, a Marine Corps lieutenant who had served in Beirut at the time of the airport bombing. Also among our ranks were an architect, a Canadian ski instructor, an Australian veterinarian, a former assistant to the prime minister of Japan, and me, Episcopal priest who had left a position at Grace Church on Tenth Street in Manhattan to pursue graduate studies in the relationship between economics and Christianity.

My wife and I had moved to Boston because Dana, toting a newly minted Ph.D. from Yale, had been hired as an assistant professor at Boston University's School of Theology. I had a choice of searching for a parish in the area or entering a doctoral program in business policy and business ethics. Figuring I could always return to the parish, I leapt into an experimental year at the West Point of corporate capitalism, the Harvard Business School.

The school felt, and understandably so, that I should learn some of the basics about business before I began doctoral work, so they placed me in the first year of the MBA program.

I barely remember what happened those first weeks. Suddenly I was yanked from the cool Gothic halls of Grace Church, where my days had been spent preaching, teaching, counseling and working with the destitute street people of New York City, and I was dropped into the world of a business school, with its perplexing courses on marketing, accounting, managerial economics and organizational behavior. Instead of relying on the language of theology—a language filled with words such as salvation, redemption, forgiveness and grace—I was abruptly required to speak with an entirely new vocabulary which consisted of phrases such as depreciation tax shield, cumulative probability distribution curve, product cannibalization, net present value and subordinated convertible debenture. Instead of pondering the apostle Paul's logic in his letter to the Romans, I found myself designing a consumer and trade promotion campaign for Vaseline Petroleum Jelly.

It was also my fortune (or misfortune, depending on whom you talk to) to belong to the first MBA class to be required to purchase individual personal computers. The previous summer, we had all been mailed archly worded letters announcing that we would be expected to buy an IBM portable computer, through the university, for a mere $3,200. At about the same time an article appeared in *The Wall Street Journal* questioning the machine's value, popularity and future prospects. A spokeswoman for IBM responded with what she considered decisive evidence of the portable's merits: the Harvard Business School was ordering 800 for its incoming students. Even I, a computer illiterate, realized that this was not an auspicious sign.

In the opening weeks of class I discovered that the business school relies exclusively on the case method to teach business skills. This means that you are confronted with a detailed account (including teams of numbers and charts) of some business problem an executive is facing. You must begin by figuring out what's going on (often the most difficult task), then somehow derive a solution, and finally prepare some remarks so that you will have something to say if you are the hapless student chosen at random to make the opening presentation the next morning. The analytical process is repeated with little variation approximately 400 times during the school year, giving rise to a famous school adage: "First they scare you to death, then they work you to death, then they bore you to death."

The business school gives tremendous weight (often 50 percent of one's grade) to classroom participation, and I realized early on that I would have to overcome my paralyzed silence. This was difficult because my classmates, who had the benefit of several years in business, were hurling words and concepts around the room with alarming and ferocious alacrity.

Even more difficult than mastering the language was the problem of what identity I should adopt in the classroom. I had made it very clear on my application that I was not leaving the ministry and that I intended to teach or return to the parish, but the moment I began classes at Harvard I became an anomaly wherever I went. At business school I was peculiar because I was a minister; with church friends and other ministers, however, I was equally peculiar because I was in business school. This tension between the life of faith and the life of business was exactly what I had come to the business school to reflect on, but it was distressing to find the tension so soon and within my own person. I found it very tricky to know how to act in class.

Once in a while I spoke up about what I thought were broader political or ethical issues raised by the cases. Was it really necessary to close this plant and throw hundreds of people out of work? Did any sane human being really want overpriced deodorant socks to be conveniently available in supermarkets? What effect might these massive shampoo-marketing efforts we were planning have on the families we had targeted? Isn't it possible that this highly profitable hospital chain might be earning money by excluding the poor? The class seemed to tolerate my outbursts but rarely supported them.

Once I tried to break out of the mold of class ethicist, just to see what it was like. We were discussing the problems of a men's cologne that was declining in popularity. I raised my hand and said, "It's all image and air anyway, so let's capture that air with a campaign built on the most expensive sort of snob appeal." The professor looked startled. "This, from a man of your background?" he said. The class laughed.

I still don't know whether he meant it as a compliment or a reproof. In any case, I never again recommended something I didn't believe in. I stuck to the role I had been granted as a liberal bellwether, a miner's canary who, as long as he didn't pipe up or keel over, certified that ethical boundaries were being respected.

With all the long hours of class, there was lots of time to look around the room and daydream. One thing that always struck me was the abnormal percentage of physically attractive people at the business school. The men are generally tall, square of jaw, and highly athletic; the women distinctively attractive and frequently preppy. Rare indeed were unshapely figures, stringy hair, nondescript faces, pasty complexions—to say nothing of disability or disease or the other signs of human mortality. The people at the business school actually looked like the people in ads for Caribbean vacations or for expensive liquor; they looked like *winners*.

During one three-day case series, we studied a cold remedy that introduced no new medical features into the marketplace and whose advertising budget would represent 60 percent of its retail price. I decided to keep quiet and see what people would say. After the second day, nine people came up to me separately to inquire why I had not yet objected to this "piece of crap." I encouraged them to speak up, but they blushed. Even one professor remarked, again privately, that the product was terrible. But in three days of class, no one openly objected.

And thus the dilemma: privately and personally the students were warm human beings, but publicly many adopted aggressive, cynical and callous styles. In the fall we saw a movie on the coal miners' strike in Harlan County, Kentucky, and the sight of the overweight miners' wives brought wave after wave of cackling derision. When, in a discussion of textile workers in England, it was revealed that a woman who had sewed for 12 years for $100 a week might lose her job, the class was almost unanimous in the feeling that she deserved to be laid off, since she was being paid too much.

Moreover, all day long the students talked about money. Discussions about money in Managerial Economics of Control (the business school's term for accounting) or Finance always had a clinical quality, as though money were a force with its own properties and principles, like electricity. At meals, though, the conversation would turn to money as something to be pursued for the freedom and pleasure it gave. People would talk about how much a person used to make, or how much someone had inherited, or how much they would earn. At one lunch students were surprised and titillated to hear that a second-year student graduating in the class of 1985 had "broken the barrier of 100 K" by landing a job with an investment bank for what turned out to be a starting salary of $140,000. One day I asked a fellow student what he most wanted to do in life. "What I most want to do is make a great deal of money," he said amiably.

It might seem unfair to generalize about the attitudes of 1,600 MBA students. Though the students as a whole were conservative, there was a smattering of liberals dispersed through the sections. Though the general attitude toward ethics was that it wasted time, there were some students who thought and said otherwise. By the end of the year, however, I came to feel that these students were the exception that proved the rule and that there was a strongly shared perspective, a faith, as it were, common to almost everyone there.

The first article of faith in the HBS doctrine was an unquestioning conviction concerning the economic and moral superiority of large-scale corporate capitalism. The basic justice and integrity of current economic arrangements were never publicly challenged. There were many corollary tenets to this central creed, notably that:

> Competition is always the most efficient means of distributing resources.

> Government is always inefficient and something to be reduced, controlled, and mocked.

> Monopolies are bad if you are on the buying end, but good if you can achieve them in your own industries (this is called building market share).

> American workers are fat, slow and inefficient, and labor unions are a destructive force.

> Poverty and unemployment are the result of inefficiency and primarily the fault of the poor and the unemployed.

> Almost any marketing or promotional campaign can be justified on the grounds that if a consumer actually buys the product, it must be to fulfill some "need."

> Individual greed always aggregates to a larger good, therefore the rabid pursuit of materialism is only a good thing.

Since the case method requires the professor to ask questions and play students' responses off each other, I often wondered how my professors really felt about these matters. Were they also so cynical? Did they endorse the primitive social Darwinism that prevailed among the MBA students?

By Christmastime I got up the nerve to visit different professors to inquire about the curriculum and about their feelings on ethics in business. Many of them, in contrast to the students, were eager to talk about the profound moral and philosophical problems in modern business. I even detected a certain frustration with the students' narrow focus.

The more I talked to the professors and listened to their comments in class, the more it seemed that they had a definite mission they were seeking to achieve through the design of the curriculum. Not only did they intend to turn out well-rounded general man-

agers, but many of them also hoped by doing so to arrest or
reverse America's decline as a manufacturing nation and world
competitor. The constant theme in the case material was that Japanese firms have outperformed American firms because they have
designed marketing programs that are more responsive to con-
sumers, organizations that are more sensitive to employees, and factories that take seriously the contributions to quality and production
offered by workers. The message to us was direct and simple:
American managers must become more attentive listeners, more
humble, more interested in the long term than the short, and more
devoted to the company's success than to their own careers.

Although this was what the curriculum stressed, the *culture* at
the business school, harking back to an earlier, more arrogant time,
emphasized the reverse. Students were graded on a forced bell
curve, which rewarded people with prior training and work experience and automatically failed the bottom 10 to 15 percent in each
class. The stereotype most admired by students was that of the
"tough, hands-on manager," someone who justifies his or her high
pay by being the crisis solver, the problem fixer and the head bash-
er. When we studied People Express (which attributed its success to
its innovative and responsive personnel policies), the students
reluctantly agreed that these policies were a good idea, but as soon
as we were confronted with an open-ended problem, many again
recommended top-down, management-directed solutions.

At no period is the emphasis on individual success and achievement more evident than in the frenzied winter mating season when
recruiters arrive on campus. Throughout the fall students rewrite
and edit their resumes, join organizations such as the Finance Club,
the Marketing Club, the Investment Banking Club and the Venture
Capital Club (in part to get their names included in special club
books), and pore over annual reports and lists of alumni in the
Career Research Center. Then the recruiters arrive and the students
begin a swirling dance of first-, second- and third-round interviews
and callbacks that lasts for three weeks. Attention is paid to the
most minute details of performance and appearance. "I was going
out the door to an interview," recounted one friend, "and my room-
mate stopped me and asked me with alarm, 'What are you doing?' I
didn't know what he was talking about. 'You can't go to an interview with a bank wearing brown shoes!' He made me change
them."

Occasionally I came to the business school in a suit because I
had appointments in town immediately after class, and each time
my sectionmates playfully inquired if I had "given in" and decided
to interview with Goldman Sachs or McKinsey. "Come on, Bob,"

one good friend of mine said, "Those consulting jobs look pretty good, don't they? Wouldn't it be fun to tell other companies what to do? Wouldn't you like to make $1,300 a week for a summer job?"

The spectacle of hundreds of students desperately searching for work was not without irony when one remembered the ease with which these same students proposed shutting plants and firing workers who had been employed for 25 years. The students, however, do not consider themselves to be in the same league (dare I say species?) as workers; they have become *managers*. Having put up as much as $30,000 for tuition, endured two years of cases and cold calls, and earned a degree from Harvard, they feel they *deserve* a job. They believe that they are now entitled to a high salary and to the unquestioned right to make decisions about other people's lives.

That pervasive sense of entitlement bothered me more than anything. It made me realize that as much as I loved being a member of Section F, as proudly as I wore my "F Troop" baseball cap, the sectional system is designed to create and reinforce a sense of managerial elitism. High pressure and close contact for nine months create bonds, and the bonds create a sense of a peer group, and the peer group forms a culture that sets it off from the rest of the world. Like those who have been through boot camp or some peculiar initiation rite, the students who survive the first year of the Harvard Business School become the members of a club and, by definition, a member of a club is a better person than a nonmember.

I came to the business school because I had stood outside of the corporate club for years and criticized it. I had criticized it in part because I did not understand what businesses actually did and because I had been on the receiving end of business activity all my life—of its products, its advertising, its pollution, its political clout. After my year at Harvard, I understood more and so I am less critical about some things. I now understand, for example, how extraordinarily difficult it is to run a business, how many complex and divergent parts—finance, marketing, sales, production distribution—have to be coordinated. And I have come to believe that there is nothing wrong and, in fact much that is good about a few people coming together, pooling their resources, and trying to provide a service or a product for which they earn a return on their investment. In other words, I have become a fan of small business.

However, the question I brought to the business school—What is the relationship between such economic activities and the Christian faith?—is going to require a good deal more work. For one thing, the question has been debated by theologians since the

beginning of the church; it is a derivative of the thorny problem of
how closely or distantly the church should participate in the institutions of the world. Over the centuries some have argued, at one
extreme, for complete withdrawal from society, whereas others
have simply baptized whatever the culture approves as good with a
sprinkling of holy water.

For the serious person of faith who commutes between a
church on Sunday and a corporate job on weekdays, who is drawn
by the hope and joy and freedom of the gospel yet must live amidst
the rules of the marketplace, such extreme answers offer little sol-
ace. Church leaders fortunate enough to have money to set aside
cannot escape the difficult question of how to invest those funds in
a manner consistent with their beliefs. And on a global level, no
person who professes that all human beings are beloved children of
the same God can be complacent in a world where hundreds of
millions live in subhuman poverty.

As the year progressed I came to realize that the most profound
question posed by a place like the Harvard Business School is a
question common to every human endeavor: What greater goal of
God are we individually and collectively called to serve in life? The
biblical logic that governs my faith says simply that human beings
can never be happy as long as they build their lives around false
gods, that is, things that seem to grant life or power but in fact cannot.

And so as a minister in a business school I found myself won-
dering all year what the school is really teaching. Some might argue
that it communicates a useful and value-free body of knowledge the
same way a school for auto mechanics communicates certain func-
tional skills. But an alternative view occurred to me when once,
during the course of the year, I returned to a gathering of the members of Grace Church and someone welcomed me back as "one of
our three seminarians who have gone off to study." Another speaker
commented, "I know we live in Orwellian times and war is peace,
but I never thought I would hear the Harvard Business School
described as a seminary. But I don't know. Maybe it's true."

*The Rev. Robert K. Massie Jr. is a candidate for the degree of Doctor of Business
Administration and he is priest-in-charge of Christ Church, Somerville, Massachusetts.*

The Ministry of the Laity:
Reflections for Study and Debate

by Neil M. Alexander

Many continue to explore the theory and practice of the ministry of the laos (the service of the people of God). It is helpful to have common points of departure as we engage in thinking and discussion. The following two articles have been prepared to resource our continuing search for understanding and confidence in our quest. You might use these articles as a basis for personal study or share them with others to elicit response and possibly debate. . . .

Pay Attention

One night my wife Leslie and I were taking a walk near our home in Nashville. We were enjoying the evening breezes after a delightful dinner at a new restaurant. As we walked, we were approached by two men carrying large shopping bags and dressed in tattered clothing.

The older of the two addressed me. "Say, buddy," he asked, "can you spare a hundred dollars?" I laughed, said "Sorry," and passed on. His request, I suppose now, was meant to suggest that a little loose change would seem easy enough to share in comparison to one hundred dollars—still, it was such a ludicrous question that it was easy for me to feel OK about saying no.

After some reflection I am no more sure about the adequacy of my response to his request than I am when I recall similar (though more modest) requests from people begging in the streets of such diverse locations as Mexico City; Haiti; Washington, D.C.; and Dublin, Ireland.

The phrase *the ministry of the laity* has a nice ring to it and invites freewheeling conversations and debates that can keep any group worth its salt busy for at least a few hours. But when I talk about the ministry of the laos—the service of the people of God—I like to sharpen the focus a bit. That focus has to do with what we can and must pay attention to in our communities and in the world.

That focus involves seeing through the eyes of God the life needs and aspirations of real people. The yearning for intimacy and trust in families, the hope for integrity and compassion in our communities. The desperate need for justice and mercy in our world. The danger is that our discussion of such topics will be lifted to levels of such high abstraction that we will mask the bite of our encounters with real people—like the man who asked if I could spare a hundred dollars. My dilemma is that in fact I actually could.

But should I? And if not at random on a busy street with one passerby who is in need—how—and with whom—and when?

Character, someone said, is what you're like when no one's watching you—or at least when you forget that others are watching you.

Robert Coles writes about such matters saying that "Dickens...was shrewd about this sort of irony in our lives...when he used the expression 'telescopic philanthropy' to describe (someone like the person) whose compassion for far off South Africa's black people (is) boundless but who could also, near at home, behave... shamelessly."

Coles notes that Jesus spent his three years of earthly ministry in everyday acts of mercy, emphasizing the importance of the concrete deed. Coles then counsels, "Let those of us who find that words come easy, and who like to play with ideas, and call the attention of others to our words and ideas, beware. Our jeopardy is real and continuing" (*New Oxford Review*, January-February 1985).

With such cautions in mind I want to suggest that the ministry of the laos is not simply a polite subject for church discussion groups. Rather it is a very serious matter involving a choice between what is good and what is bad. A matter that requires the turning of the whole of our attention to God through prayer and action. A matter of discerning direction for our human vocation as obedient and faithful servants of the living Christ. I want to suggest that evil is real and that the stakes involved in our finding and following God's will for our lives are high—matters, in fact, of life and death.

In the fifth chapter of Ephesians we read: "Look carefully then how you walk, not as unwise men (and women) but as wise, making the most of the time because the days are evil" (3:15-16).

For some of us the idea that evil and sin are realities in our world is confirmed easily through direct experience. Yet many of us are subject to popular notions that lead us to avoid thinking and talking about evil as though it were real. As though it were a force to be reckoned with that involves tremendous consequences.

A few of my co-workers gathered once to study the well-known parable of the good Samaritan. We were considering what it means to be a good neighbor in contemporary life. One in our group said that "the problem with talking about the kinds of behaviors that constitute being a good neighbor is that we run the risk of suggesting that there is such a thing as a *bad* neighbor. Actually," he said, "the opposite of doing good is more like *failing* to do good." I fear that my colleague's statement reflects a prevailing view. Somehow we find it difficult to believe that persons can and do make choices that are *bad*.

One writer has suggested that the devil embarrasses modern Christians but was indisputably real to Jesus and the early church. I am treading on dangerous ground here, since many thoughtful and knowledgeable theologians debate with some heat the "nature of evil" and its manifestations. I simply want to say that evil or "bad things" seem real enough to me and seem often enough to be the consequences of choices (personal *and* corporate) that otherwise "good people" make for a variety of reasons.

The residents of my neighborhood were awakened recently at 1:30 a.m. on a Sunday morning by the crackle of fire. We were frightened when we discovered that the garage belonging to the house next door to mine was fully engulfed in flames. Subsequent investigation by the fire marshal resulted in evidence that the fire had been maliciously set by an arsonist. It is hard for any of us involved to view this event as the result of someone who simply did something that was "not good." We do not find it hard to assert that someone, for whatever reasons, acted as a *bad* neighbor in setting that fire.

And, of course, evil does not only present itself to us in the form of individual misdeeds. Even more complex are discussions of evil which take a critical look at its corporate/social manifestations. Depending on our politics and forms of analysis we will come up with different lists of some of these social ills. I have a friend who helps sum up the idea of systemic evil by pointing to the fact that if we want to transform the conditions that cause pain and suffering in our communities and the world, we must not only be prepared to help repair the broken legs of our neighbors—we must also locate and dismantle the leg-breaking machines that are responsible for their condition!

If we could believe that hunger in Africa or Chicago was only the result of bad luck (water shortage, crop failure) and not the result of deliberate economic policies and politics; if we could believe that war between nations was simply a matter of a breakdown in "communications" and not the result of greed and calculated power plays; if we could believe that child abuse was not often related to exploitive and profitable pornographic stimulants—we might be more casual in discussing the role that human choices play in causing evil conditions to flourish.

The fact is that choices are made every day that have evil, alienating, and life-denying consequences. Some of these consequences are intensely personal, almost private in nature. They involve broken relationships between parents and children or the abuse of personal power in the workplace. Some of these consequences are decidedly public. They involve insensitive policy and practice with respect to the rights of those who are the weakest (prisoners, minorities, the poor), and our use or abuse of commonly held resources (the environment, governmental budgets).

Of course, there are choices we make daily that contribute to public or private good. Why not concentrate on these more hopeful and life-giving examples of human actions in our discussion of ministry? Because, the Christian faith calls us to a kind of ultimate honesty and reckoning that acknowledges our final and total dependence on what Thomas Merton called "an invisible and inscrutable God."

Merton suggests that "underlying all life is the ground of doubt and self-questioning which sooner or later must bring us face to face with the ultimate meaning of our life. This self-questioning can never be without. . .a sense of insecurity, of 'lostness,' of exile, of sin. It is the profound awareness that one is capable of ultimate bad faith with himself and with others" (*Contemplative Prayer*, Image Books, 1977).

The Bible is emphatic on this subject. For example, Moses speaks to us through the pages of Deuteronomy: "Today I am giving you a choice between good and evil, between life and death. If you obey the commands of the Lord your God. . .if you love God, obey God, and keep all (of) God's laws, then you will prosper and become a nation of many people. But if you disobey and refuse to listen, and are led away to worship other gods, you will be destroyed. I warn you here and now. I am now giving you the choice between life and death, between God's blessing and God's curse, and I call heaven and earth to witness the choice you make. Choose life! (Deuteronomy 30).

Authentic ministry takes seriously the reality of evil. As Christ's disciples we must take seriously our capacity to make bad choices. So where shall we look for direction; how shall we find our way along such a treacherous path? We must look not to our own resources for the saving possibility, but to God. "Pray for me," says Mother Teresa of Calcutta, "that I not loosen my grip on the hand of Jesus."

Jeremiah puts it another way. "I will give them a heart to understand that I am Yahweh, and they shall be my people and I will be their God when they return to me with all their heart" (24:7).

Encountering God—like Moses found with the burning bush—is an awesome experience. Failing to encounter God at all is a tragic experience. In the movie version of *Tribute*, Jack Lemmon plays the part of a character who is dying as the result of a terminal illness.

A friend asks how he manages to cope day-by-day with any degree of hope and expectation. "Could it be," asked the friend, "that you get your ability to cope from God?" "No," says Lemmon's character, "somehow God never caught my attention."

The pathos and tragedy of that statement have stuck with me as I have considered our spiritual quest to know and love the God who *already* knows and loves us.

A friend of mine had been a hard-driving, vigorous, no-nonsense executive. He was liked but also feared by co-workers. He was smart, determined, hard on the edges, efficient, self-contained, and all the rest. Then on a business trip he was struck by a car while crossing the street and almost died. It took over two years for him to recover the full use of his limbs. Somehow this personal crisis struck deeply, not only into his body but into his spiritual center. He came to terms with his own finiteness and with God's merciful healing of *both* body and spirit.

He was not the same. He was still smart, still efficient, still productive—but he was also softer, quieter, more caring, and more approachable. He had been opened up to experience his own pain and God's love. He was a different person. How shall we turn *our* attention to God and find the ways to live for what is good and not evil? Shall we wait for an accident or tragedy?

In his book *Contemplative Prayer*, Thomas Merton counsels that we must return to God with all our heart through prayer—including prayerful attention to the world around us. He suggests that such prayer involves opening oneself with humble and courageous exposure to what the world ignores about itself—both good *and* evil. In encountering the abyss of evil, the contemplative faces the worst, and discovers in it the hope of the best. "From the abyss there comes, unaccountably, the mysterious gift of the Spirit sent by God to make all things new, and to reestablish all things in Christ."

We must cultivate a new and deeper spiritual vision as a means of seeing life through God's sound eye—by a God-centered vocation to which we devote our hearts, our minds, our service.

We look to the ministry of Jesus for clues and direction. In Luke 4 we find the story of Jesus' address in the synagogue in Nazareth in which he reads from the book of the prophet Isaiah to proclaim his own coming to "bring good news to the poor" and "liberty to the captives."

Remember how just prior to the inauguration of Jesus' ministry he spent forty days in the desert tuning his attention to the will of God and resisting the temptations of the devil? Remember how immediately after his address in the synagogue the people scorned him and threatened to throw him off a cliff?

For Jesus, ministry was rooted in the experience of the desert, coming to terms, in a fundamental way, with obedience to the will of God even in the face of enormous temptation. He then spoke to the people using words that were deeply imbedded in their experience and sense of expectation. His message offered hope where there was despair, healing where there was brokenness. And yet, he knew that one proclaims the truth at great risk. Many would not be receptive to his message or his witness.

The late William Stringfellow noted that a great misconception about the gospel is that it is welcome in the world. Such a notion is not supported by Scripture which shows that "during Jesus' earthly ministry, no one in His family and not a single one of the disciples accepted Him, believed His vocation or loved the gospel He bespoke and embodied" (*The Witness*, May 1977).

Discerning our vocation—I am using *vocation* here to mean the central purpose and direction for our lives as God's servants—is not a casual matter. James Fenhagen addresses critical questions related to *vocation* and *discerning* the spiritual *vision* that can guide us in his helpful book, *Ministry and Solitude*. "No one becomes a 'minister,'" says Fenhagen. "Rather in trust we so open ourselves to the Spirit that Jesus Christ can express his ministry through us."

Discerning our vocation, opening ourselves to the guidance of the Spirit in forming the vision that can direct our life's choices is a crucial task in shaping the ministry of the laos—the service of the people of God.

In Romans we read, "Let your mind be remade and your whole nature thus transformed. Then you will be able to discern the will of God, and to know what is good, acceptable and perfect" (12:2).

Robert Coles tells the story of a young boy he met in his work as a psychiatrist. The boy, Bob we'll call him, was seven years old at the time. Bob's parents worked hard and long hours in building up an orange grove in Florida. They had, through effort and good fortune, become quite successful in this enterprise. They were good people who participated fully in the life of their community and Christian congregation where Bob attended Sunday school.

One day, in his second grade class at public school, Bob's teacher asked the children to describe what they thought they'd like to be when they became adults. Bob said, "I'm not sure—but one thing I don't want to be is rich." Bob's teacher chuckled at this response and asked Bob why not. He replied that he had learned that it wasn't good to be rich in his Sunday school class. "Oh, Bob," said the teacher, "what on earth could have given you that idea?" Bob reported that they had been studying the Bible and learned that it was harder for a rich man to get into heaven than it was for a camel to fit through the eye of a needle.

His teacher, realizing that Bob had misinterpreted a complex biblical understanding, reported this conversation to his parents. They began to note that Bob was often questioning their lifestyle as orange grove owners. He couldn't understand why his friends (mostly children of migrant workers) lived in such relative poverty and didn't have the same food, clothing, and toys that he did. His behavior grew increasingly rebellious and resistant to his parents' attempt to explain these matters and they finally sought psychiatric treatment for Bob.

I have some sympathy for Bob's parents. Looking to the Bible and to the guidance of the Spirit for direction in our Christian voca-tion *can* lead to some disturbing consequences. The stakes involved in acting out our ministry as the people of God are high, and not without cost in a world that often fails to take the Bible and its claims on our attention seriously.

One reason it is so important to focus on brokenness in the world, when reflecting on our ministry as the people of God, is that the world encourages us to ignore or gloss over the disparity between the way things are and the way God wills them to be. Faithful disciples pay attention to the loneliness of children yearn-ing for the love and affection of parents who are too busy and too tired to provide it. The world says they'll get over it and turns on the TV. Faithful disciples pay attention to the alienation of persons with physical and mental disabilities by taking pains to help them feel included and loved. The world often views such persons as a burden, since success and efficiency are the measures of worth and the gods we worship. Faithful disciples pay attention to broken mar-riages, broken promises, and broken hopes. The world shrugs its shoulders and suggests that it's all we can manage to look out for our own interests.

"What people see is an indication of what they care about and can care about," writes Craig Dykstra in *Vision and Character* (Paul-ist Press, 1981). "It is an indication of the depth and breadth of their compassion.... Acts of attention do not leave us unchanged. When other people or things or ideas are received by us through our realistic perception of them, we are not left as we were."

The ministry of the laos involves paying attention—attention, on the one hand, to the hopes and cries of creation—to the people and institutions that make up the fabric of our lives close at home and far away. On the other hand, it involves attention to the call of God laying claim to our hearts and minds, to our devotion and our service.

How will paying attention to God and God's world help us know what to do—help us know how to act? Many of us feel bombarded already by myriad issues and needs.

It is helpful to note that many of the persons we might cite as faithful witnesses of extraordinary faith do not view themselves as courageous, brave, or heroic. People like the mother of a child killed by a drunk driver who organized an effective national movement to change public policy and protect children everywhere; people like the neighbor who wouldn't take no for an answer from the local human services agency which claimed there was no way to provide food for the hungry elderly woman who lived next door; people who refuse to give in to fear or a sense of powerlessness and work for peace and an end to the arms race. These are real people of character and determination. Ask them and they will tell you they are not heroic. Rather, their hearts and minds give them no choice but to act to make a difference!

What sets such persons apart is: (1) they are willing to pay attention to their own pain and the pain of others; (2) they are willing to acknowledge that the "way things are" is not good enough; (3) they listen intently to the voice of God calling to them from deep within their heart—compelling them to act and make a difference. Ask them and they'll tell you they cannot predict the outcome of their labors, cannot be sure their efforts will make a difference. But the urgency and calling they experience lead them to take first one step, and then another, and then another.

Discerning God's will involves turning our attention and service to the tasks toward which the Spirit leads us, while acknowledging the presence of evil that stands in the way. Discernment involves distinguishing what is good from what is bad by testing—taking one step and then another under the guidance that comes with critique by our neighbors and through devotion to the disciplines of our faith.

I know a homemaker in Virginia who has helped parents of mentally retarded children band together for support. I know a farmer in Kansas who leads marriage growth sessions for his neighbors. I know an Internal Revenue Service auditor in Nashville who works in a downtown soup kitchen. I know a woman in rural Mississippi who has organized a community garden project for low income people there. I know a retired educator in New York who is tirelessly devoted to building understanding of the issues and commitment to action to reduce the threat of nuclear war. *You* know people of God who, by paying attention to groans of the earth and to the call of the Spirit, have found their vocation of ser-vice—people who are making a difference in the world.

What are *you* paying attention to? What are the hopes and hurts, aspirations and struggles of the people in your home, your neigh-borhood, your school, or place of work? Where in all the world are the leg-breaking machines that need to be dismantled? Which *one* will you confront?

What are you paying attention to? Are you engaging in the means of grace through Bible study and prayer? Through regular worship and acts of service? Listening to discern the still small voice of God calling from within your heart—leading you to fulfill your vocation as a Christian disciple?

Henri Nouwen has written, "As prayer leads us into the house of God and God's people, so action leads us back into the world to work there for reconciliation, unity and peace. . . . It is a confident expression of the truth that in Christ, death, evil, and destruction have been overcome" (*Sojourners*, June 1985).

The ministry of the laos is intentional service by the people of God, paying attention to God and God's world. What are you paying attention to?

Making the World Fit to Live In

A fruitful discussion of the ministry of the laos has less to do with the role of the laity in tension with the role of clergy than it has to do with the vocation *all* of us have as servants of the living Christ.

I want now to extend our thinking about ministry. In doing so I am probably testing the limits of your patience and may leave you thinking of me as George Will said of Walter Mondale during the 1984 presidential campaign. "Mondale," said Will, "is a Houdini-in-reverse: From any position of safety he can swiftly escape into dan-ger" (*Newsweek*, July 16, 1984).

Yet, consider the following from the eighth chapter of Romans: "So then my brothers and sisters, we have an obligation, but it is not to live as our human nature wants us to. For if you live accord-ing to your human nature, you are going to die; but if by the Spirit you put to death your sinful actions, you will live."

Susan is sixteen and pregnant. She is just beginning to grow up physically and mentally and now she is about to become a parent herself. She looks forward to the birth of her child. Her own life has been marred by a sad and anxious childhood. Her mother was demanding and brutal; her father, cold and moody.

"All I want is a baby, then I can forget the rest of the world, and try to be nice to her, and make up for what I missed," she says. "There is no one in the world who cares about me. . . . God must have felt sorry for me and sent this baby to me."

We've all heard the statistics. The rate of teenage pregnancies in the United States has increased by tragic proportions. We debate about what to do. Some talk about medical solutions such as birth control techniques. Some talk about educational solutions such as sex education programs in the schools. Some talk about systemic changes such as addressing drug abuse, exploitive portrayals of sex in the media, and economic conditions like unemployment which all seem to be causal factors in the increased rate of teenage pregnancies.

Robert Coles suggests we look even deeper as we consider the dilemma. He tells the story of one fifteen-year-old pregnant girl in Atlanta. "Once I heard a young woman plead for 'someone to talk to.' She needed 'counseling,' we all thought. But she added this: 'Someone to talk to so I'll be able to find myself, and know what I believe, and what I musn't do, because it's wrong.' She said 'wrong'—not 'costly,' not 'unnecessary,' 'medically harmful,' not avoidable" (*New Oxford Review*, July-August 1984). Just wrong. She was not asking for generalized attention to the problem of teenage pregnancies—but for specific attention that would help her know how to live and make daily choices.

There is a story attributed to Garrison Keillor who hosts the delightful Public Radio program, " A Prairie Home Companion." No doubt it has changed some in numerous retellings. It is said that Keillor once told a story about a contemporary of his who had written saying his life had fallen apart. It seems that his friend was a scholar specializing in ancient languages who found an appointment teaching dead languages at a small midwestern college soon after completing his doctoral work. Twelve years later the college determined that there really wasn't much demand for a chair in dead languages and closed out his position on the faculty. He was now serving as associate dean of admissions, a task for which he had little commitment.

Keillor's friend became depressed and discouraged. His life was dull and, now in his mid-forties, he saw no future for his chosen field of study—his life's work. He was lonely, defeated, and felt powerless. His new work assignment led to representing his college at a regional meeting of admissions officers at an out-of-state location. While attending the conference he met some lively folks who were planning a two-day "escape" of frolicking fun at a nearby resort. He was anonymous at the conference. No one would miss him and he was sorely tempted to nurse his wounds with a couple of days of illicit fun away from his assigned task.

The moment of decision came and he wondered what he should do. There was nothing preventing him from choosing to join the crowd for some good times in an otherwise dull and disappointing period of his life. And then he thought, "If I do this now, somewhere a father at the same moment may decide to give way to his anger and strike a child; if I do this now, somewhere a businesswoman may decide to cheat on her expense account; if I do this now, somewhere a neighbor may decide to ignore a cry for help."

Perhaps Keillor's friend was simply rationalizing and over-simplifying the negative effects one small, almost insignificant choice could have on the delicate fabric that holds our lives and communities together. Or, perhaps he was confirming an understanding of the importance of choice that Reinhold Niebuhr wrote about. Niebuhr suggests that our freedom to choose gives the capacity to relate ourselves to the eternal, to the "things that abide" which are "faith, hope, and love."

Faith, he says, is the capacity to transcend all changes in history and look to the ultimate *source* of historical reality; hope is the capacity to transcend all changes in history and look to the ultimate *end* that fulfills all history. "Love," says Niebuhr, "is the capacity to recognize the social substance of human existence, and to realize that the unique self is intimately related to *all* human creatures" (*Context*, February 15, 1985).

Perhaps the disillusioned professor of dead languages was choosing to recognize the social substance of human existence. Perhaps the pregnant teenager in Atlanta was looking for help in finding the threads that hold the fabric of our lives together as we groan from deep within our hearts for the knowledge and the means by which we might faithfully serve God.

Attention to the ministry of the laos—*the intentional service of the people of God*—involves earnest concern for the choices involved in the context of our day-to-day life. It is in the home and neighborhood, in the daily struggles and joys of human experience in the world that God's people find themselves confronted with the question, "How then shall we live?"

Soon after World War II, Harry Emerson Fosdick compiled a set of sermons under the intriguing title *On Being Fit to Live With* (Harper & Brothers, 1946). His theme was that life in post-war America was a time of great peril and great opportunity. He wrote that our destiny rested not with our own technological and social achievements, but with the choices we would make in looking deep within our hearts for the "still small voice" of God, for living as obedient and faithful servants.

Fosdick did not minimize the importance that individual choices for good play in shaping our world's context—a context which he believed, and we have now come to know, was made decidedly global by the splitting of the atom.

In one of his sermons he marveled at the courage and power evidenced in the prodigal son's return home. He concluded by urging his readers to pass "over from being a part of (humankind's) disease to being part of the cure." "Whenever that happens," he said, "it makes a difference to the whole race. No little thing that Prodigal did when he came home, not little for himself nor his father, nor for the world. That event is still one of (humankind's) unforgettables." "God grant," says Fosdick, "that it may happen here today, for in the long run everything depends on enough people who are part of the answer." Everything depends on people who are striving to be fit to live with and striving to make the world fit to live in—people choosing, intentionally and purposefully; people acting confidently and courageously in the ordinary situations of daily life, as well as in the global arenas of human history.

When we think of the ministry of the laos in this way, it becomes strikingly clear how important the nurture and prodding, the support and empowering of the faith community is to the fostering of disciples. The subject areas for our attention to the ministry of the laity, then, are not first and foremost the role of lay leadership in our congregations or connectional structures; the participation of the laity in Bible study, worship, and church governance; or the role of church members in special programs and projects of mission and outreach.

All of these are *means*, not *ends*. All of these are part of creating the environment, the climate, and the foundation for the formation and support of a vital commitment and confidence that will help the people of God become fit to live with and build a world fit to live in. When our church institutions and programs are mistakenly held up as *the* most important and critical arenas for faithful living, we sap energy rather than release it. We divert attention for the tasks of discipleship rather than helpfully direct it.

Martin Marty tells the story of James Crumley, Jr., a bishop in the Lutheran Church in America. Crumley was representing his church at a meeting of the Lutheran World Federation in Budapest, a very important meeting. While there, he received word that his brother-in-law, who had been his mentor, pastor, and friend, had died.

Crumley could make it to the funeral if he took the one seat available on a plane leaving before the conference ended. He did so and was roundly criticized for neglecting his duties in behalf of the church.

This led Crumley to write the following to his constituents: "I believe it to be a genuine spirituality that underscores how only I can fulfill my role in my family. It is the place above all others where God has made me unique. No one else can fill the place for me where I relate to parents, brothers, spouse and children. Only I am Bob's son, Annette's husband, Frances' father. Here above all other human relationships do I have a particular identity. Someone else will be pastor to the people to whom I was pastor; someone else will be a bishop of the church. But no one else will ever fill my place in my family relationships. . . . Faith urges me to give whatever is necessary to nurture, strengthen, and build those relationships. That takes time—time to love, to serve, to enjoy, to celebrate, to mourn—together" (*Context*, February 15, 1985).

We are first and foremost members of the human family, created and loved by a merciful God. Some will disagree, but I am confident that this is true even of bishops! The laos—the people of God—are citizens of the world and its nations; they are neighbors to others in their communities and members of immediate and/or extended families. When people move to a new community they do not often first find a church to which they can belong, but rather a home they can afford, a job, and a school where they will live out the dailiness of their lives. *These* are the arenas, the settings, the contexts to which they are called to bring the witness of reconciliation, mercy, justice, and peace. *Then* they find a church which will *nurture* and *support* them in their living and serving. We who have great investments in the life and vitality of the institutional church often confuse these matters and imply in our actions that church membership and involvement are *the* key measurements of Christian faithfulness.

Bill Diehl, a strong voice for re-imaging our understandings of the ministry of the laity, tells stories about the struggles lay persons face as they grapple with the questions of allegiance and commitments, particularly with respect to their service in their homes and communities. The daily aspects of their living and witness are often in tension with the legitimate demands and needs for their service in the institutional church.

In one of his books, perhaps it was *Thank God It's Monday*, Diehl tells about a woman who had been active in lay leadership roles, including serving on the administrative board of her local church. She had grown increasingly concerned about the quality of public education in her community. Her sense of duty and calling led her to campaign successfully for a term on the local school board. She reported that a curious thing happened when she informed other church leaders that she would not be able to continue her involvement with her congregation's administrative board. *People were actually angry with her!* She found that many were disapproving and she got the clear message that she was somehow being unfaithful to her church by devoting herself to these broader "public matters."

Those of us (both clergy and laity) who have experienced a deepening of faith and a structure for our witness through congregational and connectional church programs may be at some disadvantage. We may find it particularly difficult to understand why so many laity get the feeling that what the church wants most is active and invested members, while offering little attention to *their* faithful witness in *other* settings. Certainly we do not mean this to be so. But every time I think critics of what is described as an inward and self-absorbed church are overstating their case, I recall discussions in a local council on ministries for which I served as chairperson for a time. We were angry, not just disappointed, and judgmental, not just concerned, about why a good number of our members failed to show up for our bi-monthly family night dinner programs.

Somehow, we who had worked so hard to plan these events could not bring ourselves to believe that other family and individual pursuits might make just as genuine a claim on our fellow members' time. None of us ever said so, but I wonder now if, circling somewhere around in our thinking, there wasn't the notion that church program involvement was the *real* measure of an individual's devotion to God.

Clearly there are vital congregational and connectional ministries of caring, teaching, justice, and proclamation that need and invite the participation of the people of God. Anyone who has been touched by the good works of a lay visitation group, by dedicated Sunday school teachers, by a hard-working choir, or by the example of leaders of social action efforts, will not minimize the crucial role of church programs in giving form and expression to vital discipleship. Most of us would find our lives impoverished indeed, if it had not been for good church folk who cared about such "institutional" matters as church growth and extension, lay involvement in worship, and lay leadership in church governance and mission.

But I am not suggesting the dismantling of church programs. Rather, I want to try to keep clear a distinction between *means* and *ends*. All of our programs, all of our projects, all of our efforts must be directed toward faithful response to our common call as people of God in the world. As important as congregational program, membership, and volunteer statistics are, they must not be confused with the most significant means of measuring congregational effectiveness. These are to be found by examining the quality of life experienced by *all* people in the communities our churches and their members serve.

This is, of course, a much more difficult idea to live out than it is to affirm. As institutional leaders, we know how much is yet undone and needed within our congregations, districts, conference and general church structures. And, we desperately need the presence, the gifts and the investments of greater numbers of people to meet those needs. Yet, as James Fenhagen writes, this focus on institutional achievement can "cause compulsive overwork, competitiveness. . .chronic unease. . .and make it difficult to affirm ministries outside the life of the parish because our institutional needs for success are so strong" (*Ministry and Solitude*, Seabury, 1984).

With all of this in mind, I want to share a list of ten principles that I believe are critical starting points for shaping our efforts at all levels of the church in fostering the ministry of the laity—the intentional service of the people of God.

1. Congregations must place *more* emphasis and effort on programs and support for the ministry of disciples of Jesus Christ in their *scattered* witness than in their gathered identity and fellowship as believers.

2. Our programs and leadership of congregations must become more effective and visible in their efforts to demonstrate knowledge of, and attention to, the *daily contexts* of work, play, school, home, and community life. *These* are the places where people spend the greatest portion of their lives; *these* are the places where their *particular* witness is so important and needed.

3. The mission of persons as *individuals* in all manner of coalitions and partnerships is of the utmost importance. Fostering *individual* witness and mission is of at least equal, if not greater, importance than our more common attention to the corporate witness of our congregations and connectional structures.

4. The evaluative measures used to test the adequacy of our efforts must be found not in the vitality of congregational programs but in *more* individuals exhibiting courage, compassion, and competence in addressing the hurts and hopes of their communities and the world.

5. The cultivation and enhancement of *personal visioning* to give direction for the fulfillment of each person's God-given vocation is a fundamental responsibility of the congregation—and must be fostered through new and vigorous efforts in our programming.

6. Annual conference and district structures must provide help for congregations as they initiate, test, and adapt *community-based* programs that provide *starting points* and ongoing *support* for enabling intentional service by the laity. Yet our programs must not hold our members captive to the support of institutional projects when their personal vision calls them to embark on new and different tasks.

7. Lay and clergy leadership must develop specific and long-term strategies for balancing the need of congregations to draw upon the time and resources of lay leadership in sustaining church programs while at the same time working to *release* leadership and resources for the ministry of the laity in their communities and the world. Such strategies will need to be made on the basis of a realistic assessment of the limits of time and energy that are available to persons seeking to fulfill multiple family, work, and community roles.

8. Congregations must make renewed and vigorous efforts to provide the settings for conversation, support, guidance, and accountability as persons discover and pursue their worldly vocation. The development of a comprehensive offering of small groups is a critical component of this work in congregations of all sizes.

9. Church leadership must learn to talk about the distinctive aspects of both "being" and "doing," without settling for a muddled compromise that says simply that both aspects of our spiritual development are interdependent. Related to this concern for differentiation in our approach to spiritual disciplines is our need to be effective in advocating for the "*sending*" role of congregations. Through their *sending* functions, congregations prepare and support individuals for their scattered witness—highlighting and celebrating individual efforts beyond the institution as though they were matters of intense congregational interest.

10. All levels of the church must place new emphasis on *changing* the language patterns which reinforce images that suggest that a minister is an ordained or diaconal professional and that the words *the Body of Christ* are synonymous only with the gathered church.

Some may view these principles as rather tame and easy to execute. I doubt that such is the case. I would plead for vigorous debate and profound attention in considering the implications of these principles in our planning and institutional life.

Take, for instance, just two from the list. The first calls for *more* emphasis to be placed on the scattered witness of Christian disciples than on the gathered identity of the faith community. That would mean that the women elected to the school board would be supported in her community service as a *first* priority of congregational life—rather than made to feel that she was somehow failing in her religious commitments. Does your congregation do that for its members?

A second example involves the tenth principle which calls for new care in our use of terms such as *minister* and *the Body of Christ*, which tend to limit rather than illuminate our understandings of the ministry of the laity. Serious efforts in this regard would involve care in the use of language similar to what we have learned relative to racist and sexist terminology—which, though sometimes thought to be only innocent patterns of speech, have been experienced as alienating and hurtful by large numbers of persons. We have learned that language plays an important role not only in reflecting our thinking but in *shaping* it. A measure of our willingness to give renewed importance to the ministry of the laity might even include a major rewriting of *The Book of Discipline* which is filled with inadvertent usages of language which seem to dilute our understanding that by baptism we are *all* called into ministry of Christian discipleship. Whom do you call "minister" in your congregation?

The tensions between attention to our gathered identity, on the one hand, and our scattered witness, on the other, require serious reflection.

Taking seriously the ministry of the laos—the intentional service of the people of God—is not a tame and diversionary activity for our congregations or connectional structures. Personal witness in our communities can have far-reaching social consequences.

Ruby Bridges was six years old when she single-handedly integrated a previously all-white New Orleans elementary school. For weeks she and one (very reluctant) white teacher were the only persons inside William Frantz school. Outside each morning as she arrived and each afternoon as she left, white parents and youth shouted profanities and threats.

"I don't know where that little girl gets the courage," said her teacher, in bewildered admiration. "I watch her walking with those federal marshals, and you can't help but hear what the people say to her. They're ready to kill her. They call her the worst names imaginable."

Ruby's teacher learned to respect the little girl's courage and determination to do what she thought was right. "There was a time, at the beginning, that I thought she wasn't too bright, you know, and so that was why she could be so brave on the street. But she's a bright child and she learns well. She knows what's happening, and she knows they *could* kill her.... But she keeps coming here, and she told me the other day that she feels sorry for all of them, and she's praying for them. Can you imagine that?"

When asked how she managed to face the ugly crowds day after day, Ruby said she simply couldn't forget "what her 'granny' told her—that if she prayed, God would listen, and give her the strength she needed" (*New Oxford Review*, March 1985).

Anyone looking for the social consequences of a scattered Christian witness and service might want to take note. Most of us can remember the days of New Orleans school desegregation. And now, that city has a black mayor. I wonder how we'd calculate how much Ruby's witness contributed to making that social transformation possible?

The ministry of the laos—the intentional service of the people of God—is marked by intense attention to pain, by a belief that the "way things are" just isn't good enough, and by equally intense attention to the stirrings of the heart and mind, listening for the still small voice of God calling us into faithful action.

The ministry of the laos takes seriously our need to make choices for good and not evil, so that we might, under the guidance of the Spirit, live so that we are indeed *fit to live with* and so that *the world may be fit to live in*.

The ministry of the laos is concerned with the realities and settings of everyday life—with the relationships and struggles that make up the greatest portion of our lives—and seeks to close the gap between the way things are and the way God wills them to be.

The ministry of the laos is rooted in prayer—nurtured by the community of faith—and yet scattered in its witness. When congregations teach and admonish, encourage, celebrate, and send disciples forth for service, the ministry of the laity comes alive and brings hope and healing to a groaning earth.

In the sixth chapter of Isaiah he speaks with fear and trembling, for he has seen the Lord of hosts and knows how inadequate and wanting he is in the face of such divine mercy and power. And yet, when the Lord asks, "Whom shall I send, and who will go for us?" into the world, Isaiah answers...

"Here am I! Send me."

God is calling us—*all* of us right now. How will *we* answer?

Neil M. Alexander, formerly executive for the Section on Ministry of the Laity, currently serves as the chief executive for Discipleship Resources and the General Board of Discipleship's Unit for Communication and Interpretation, the United Methodist Church.

Saturday's Ministries

by Mark Gibbs

The laity are accustomed to hearing these days demands that religion be more than a Sunday affair, and that we should bring our Christian faith into our work and jobs. We also hear, with a less certain note, the refrain that somehow or other we have to develop Christian responsibilities and ministries in national and international politics. Fair enough. But in the last quarter of the twentieth century, at least in the moderately affluent countries of Europe and North America, there is some danger of the churches slowly developing some kind of mission to the structures of industry—and then finding that there is nobody in the plants and factories to talk to. The machines have taken over, and the employees are out fishing or watching television.

Reports of the spread of automation are often exaggerated: it will take a little longer than the futurists thought to replace human beings in many production plants (and longer still in countries like Britain where the unions are likely to be powerful and awkward). But it is certainly time that the churches took a thoughtful look at the growth of leisure, at what Christian people are doing with those parts of their lives that are no longer spent in a grim routine of "sleep, work, eat," with perhaps Sundays and a few public holidays to relieve life until old age or early death. Very many people in Europe now have four weeks' vacation and six or seven three-day weekends each year, genuine possibilities for some study leave, and a reasonable pension at or before age 65. Both the working day and its demands on human energy and physical strength have shrunk. A minority of people find great satisfaction in their paid work, and often work long, too-long hours—like politicians, business executives and many clergy. A considerable majority of the population find their main satisfactions in life quite outside their working lives, in all sorts of personal, family and neighborhood relationships and activities. They live in and for their leisure time.

Leisure Is Not Just Extra Time

"Leisure" needs a little defining. The literature on the subject uses various jargon terms, such as "disposable time," "spare time," "personal time." It is not just a matter of "time on your hands": The unemployed soon find endless spare time a burden rather than a benefit. Leisure time is: *spare time available, plus at least a certain amount of spare energy and money with which to enjoy it*. There are almost infinite variations in human circumstances: some men and women may need very little money with which to enjoy their spare time, others clearly have sports or hobby interests which do require a bit of spare cash (though not as much as the sports and entertainment industries would have us think). But in the spectrum of leisure opportunities, neither the unemployed poor with too much time and no spare money, nor the frantically overbusy executive with $200,000 a year but no time to enjoy it, are to be envied.

What is new in history, and potentially a very blessed thing indeed, is that many ordinary people now have enough spare time and enough spare income to enjoy a considerable amount of leisure. They may not have quite the lifestyle of the European aristocracy before 1914, who were sometimes blessed and very often corrupted by their extraordinarily privileged position, in that they did not have to work for a living. But compared with all past generations in human history, and compared with millions of their fellow human beings still trapped in poverty, they—we—have the incredible privilege of a good deal of spare time and some resources with which to enjoy it. This is something to be put to the credit side of the 20th century.

Leisure, Too, Is To Be Examined

It has to be said bluntly that this new side of human existence has come under the scrutiny of the Gospel, like everything else. I shall never forget the furious comment from one of my students when I claimed this. He said something like, "For God's sake, keep religion out of Saturday night!" And we can easily understand why he was disturbed: he came out of a narrow Christian tradition which had in the past spoiled Sunday with negative censoriousness. He was rightly concerned lest Saturday should be ruined in the same way. We can consider this kind of false puritanism (that is what it is) in a moment. But we must nevertheless hold to the great truth that God calls us to a first-class style of life in *everything* we do, whether it is our worship or our work or our sports and entertainments and holidays, our eating and drinking and loving. Nothing is exempt, until the hour of our death.

This great truth we must accept. But we must immediately distinguish between the demands of the Gospel upon us, and the transient, trivial codes which different religious fashions or cultures or classes try to impose upon us. There is plenty of room for variety and for argument here: most of even the strictest Evangelicals today would horrify our 19th century ancestors by their weekend dress and manners and music. As Bishop E. R. Wickham of Manchester has so often said: The Christian life is never an unexamined life. But the result of placing various leisure time and leisure expenditures before the Lord does not mean that he will always say NO to them! It does mean that we accept that we are *accountable* for them, that sometimes, because we are a people on pilgrimage and with much work to do, we have to deny ourselves many perfectly "legitimate" leisure activities. Also, especially when we are young, we need to watch that we keep our Christian freedom sometimes to join with and sometimes to stand apart from current trends and fashions in leisure life, in vacations, in fashion clothes and cars and consumer gadgets. Especially we must understand the advertising traps which are set to get us entangled in unsatisfying patterns of Saturday living and expenditure. It is no part of our Christian obedience to fall for clever commercials for products or activities "which everybody is enjoying this year." (And many good, pious suburban families, who would never go to Las Vegas or serve gin and tonics in their homes, are gluttons for the latest consumer gadgets.)

Standards In Leisure Living

This matter of culture and class standards has to be examined carefully. Christians have been so censorious about other people's pleasures that one is tempted to adapt St. Augustine's famous saying and simply hold that we should love God, and buy what we like, or, love God and travel where we like. Matters of Christian aesthetics are so confused, and there has been so much stupid intolerance in the past, that many will think it ill behooves a middle-class English intellectual to say anything more. Nevertheless, I am sure that more must be said, and more must be discovered.

For though we ought to have a wide range of acceptance for all kinds of leisure activities, including many which we should personally never dream of undertaking or trying to enjoy, it is still true that not all human activities are equally valuable. It may be much more difficult than in the past to assess the relative value of singing

in the *St. Matthew Passion* or in a pop group. No doubt some leisure activities are better done badly than not at all. It is not easy to
distinguish between cultural standards and middle-class hang-ups
about "vulgarity." (How alienated many of us are from blue-collar
Christians, to our mutual loss.) But I hold strongly that problems of
cultural values are to be struggled with and argued about, not to be
swept under the carpet because they are difficult or embarrassing to
discuss. To do that is in fact an offense against our humanity, as
well as our faith; and when so many secular guides have given up
the fight to discover true standards in leisure activities in the name
of a spurious cultural tolerance, we Christians have to watch whether we are joining them.

All this is said not at all to destroy the wonderful possibilities for
joy and pleasure in our leisure time. It is simply to hope that under
God we prepare ourselves and our children for great blessings and
opportunities there as in our Saturday ministries. In the same way I
hope that what I say now will not be taken as a last, subtle, spoil-
sport attack on leisure life. I am myself something of a workaholic,
and I know the temptations to deny oneself even the minimum of
leisure and holidays necessary for healthy personal and spiritual
life, at least in "normal" times.

But sometimes, and for many Christians, the times are not normal. This is obviously true in days of war or of civil emergency.
Today Christians in South Africa or in Latin America may have to
abandon their usual life-styles, and give up holidays and amuse-
ments and many of the good things which in a way are their human
"right" to enjoy. And there is a sense in which something of the
same self-denial may be asked of some of us, for at least some part
of our lives. In many churches the number of active, committed
Christians is rather small. The situation is critical; the work of ministry and mission is dwindling, the clergy are desperately over-
strained. It may therefore be, in all Christian liberty, that, as in past
centuries, we may have to deny ourselves time off, and money for
vacations, and even leisure expenses for our children, because it
seems right to use this time and energy and income for urgent
Christian responsibilities. We must be free to do this. But we must
watch always that we do not easily condemn, as former church people often condemned, those fellow believers who feel free to
decide differently.

PART II

Living with the Incomplete

There is a sense in which the ministry of the laity is inevitably tied to a sense of living with the incomplete, the dis-ease of the unfinished business, the awareness that "There is more to be done than I am doing, but this is the best that I can do now."

Or is it?

The ministers of the laity wrestle with the principalities and powers. They walk by faith—often where no one has ever walked before.

Joan Irving is such a pioneer. She works as the administrator to develop a certified hospice in Cayuga County in the state of New York, and she is working to sensitize us all to respect the emotional needs—as well as the physical needs—of the mentally retarded. This article is her public testimony before a public forum on New York's four-year plan on aging. Next she will tackle the issue of the isolation of federal prisoners with AIDS.

Next is a story on confronting the national security state told in an interview of Margie and John Gilbert by Robert L. DeWitt, senior contributing editor of The Witness magazine and Mary Lou Suhor, editor.

John Finn is an environmental engineer in Massachusetts who believes that waste dumps represent sin born of greed, ignorance, and uncaring, and that Christians are called to respond to such brokenness, and to care for the earth.

The next brief piece is an example of a lay person acting out of a deep love of a human being. He used no "religious" terminology. He acted in the highest calling of his profession, and years later the memory of what he had done illuminated a theological doctrine for one who remembered it.

The multifaceted nature of the ministry of a lay person is illustrated by Nell Braxton Gibson's article. For her, ministry is responding to the moment, not counting the costs, not chalking up credits.

William Diehl narrows the focus to one place—the marketplace. He is troubled by the assumption that a Christian cannot be in business. He sees in such an assumption a distorted notion of the world and a misunderstanding of basic Christian doctrine.

A Ministry with
the Developmentally Disabled

by Joan Irving

Editor's Introduction: *New York State has a four-year plan to enhance programs for the aging. The public was invited to address the issues through a series of forums across the state, before the plan was made final. Out of 29 objectives, Ms. Irving chose one that addressed the mentally disabled.*

Objective: *To improve services for older developmentally disabled persons in cooperation with the office of Mental Retardation and Developmental Disabilities. There is need to demonstrate successful methods of integrating older developmentally disabled persons into the network of aging services.*

Due to increased medical knowledge, this segment of the population now lives longer; many become senior citizens.

Approximately ten years ago, the state began emptying the institutions into foster home care and day care programs which, though philosophically well-conceived, were not well supported in training and ancillary services. They are just now beginning to bring their performance in line with their purposes.

The great goal in such programs is "appropriate behavior." Be neat, clean, quiet, cheerful so you can eat at a restaurant, work at service jobs, etc. (How often I hear complaints tht they are disruptive in church—talking, hugging, singing off key!)

Any mentally retarded adult who has lived through fifty years has suffered multiple losses—not just deaths, but moves, separations, loss of functions—with little or no attention to the need to grieve so healing can take place. We have dealt somewhat better of late with the physical needs, but we have been very slow to recognize the emotional needs. Mentally retarded does not mean emotionally retarded!

Testimony presented at Public Forum on the New York State Four-Year Plan on Aging, June 3, 1987

My name is Joan Irving and I am working as the administrator to develop a certified hospice in Cayuga County. I had prepared a comment for today relative to the increased need for home health aides to cover the expansion of health care services in the home environment. However, the event I shared yesterday is so dominant in my mind, I cannot help but share that experience with you instead.

Bill died on Friday. He was buried yesterday. In his dying, he taught many of us things we have been slow to understand and showed us how much more we have to learn. Bill was an adult, in his late 50s, with Down's Syndrome. He died of complications from cancer of the gall bladder.

I first met Bill a couple of months ago. I was visiting another patient at the hospital when I heard a surgeon in the corridor explaining to Bill's foster mother that his cancer proved to be inoperable, that Bill had a short time to live and that he had not told him he was going to die because he was sure Bill would not understand. All this was said in a loud voice that Bill and the rest of the floor could not help but hear. In later weeks, the family physician became very angry because we told Bill he was going to die (he already knew it) and, even if he had not, the surgeon had announced it. Bill needed space and friends to share this with. Mental retardation does not mean absence of emotions any more than it means deafness. Our medical community needs help in understanding the needs of the dying once curative attempts are abandoned.

Bill had fine nursing care while there was skilled nursing to be done, but the nurses on the oncology floor had little or no experience with the developmentally disabled. They could not understand his speech and so did not linger to visit or comfort him. As we have more adults—indeed seniors—who are mentally retarded, we must teach their care-givers how to communicate with them by other than verbal means.

Bill attended the Intensive Services Program and the staff turned to me for help. I have been doing a series of inservice programs for the counselors and family caregivers of the elderly mentally retarded in grief and bereavement counseling. When I greet a room full of these bright, fresh, young professionals who work so well with the retarded, I am always impressed with how far away death must seem to them personally and how crucial as well as difficult it is to help them deal with their own mortality so they can be of real help to the increasing members of elderly in their care.

Bill's counselors at ISP began immediately to visit him, to take him photos and a collage celebrating the special memories of his life and the talents he had shared. They arranged for developmentally disabled friends to visit, were planning a party and hoping to bring him home to an Intermediate Care Facility to die so that others could more easily be with him. These wonderful young people do a special job with the retarded but needed help and direction in supporting the dying and grieving. Until recently, we have not felt this need.

Bill's natural family had institutionalized him years ago and had not been part of his life. They did not know how to connect with him now. Bill's foster mother was grieving hard and was directing the natural grief response of anger towards the natural family, the doctors, and the counselors. She is a retired person herself. Mortality is not an abstract issue for her personally. She needs help to accept and understand her own mortality if she is going to be a Family Care Giver for retarded seniors.

And so, yesterday two young staff members and I took John, Bill's friend and foster brother of many years, to say goodbye. The natural family had somewhat reluctantly agreed for us to come and his foster mother, tied up in her anger, had declined to join us. At the funeral home, John taught us all; he talked tenderly to "my friend Bill boy," stroked his hair, held his hand, kissed him, checked out the rosary, put a flower in the coffin. His responses were natural and honest—"He's asleep?" "No, he's dead." "He'll get up soon?" "No, we won't see him again. We must say goodbye now." "Oh, time to say goodbye?"

A simple service was said at the funeral home. We all went to the cemetery for the interment. John watched the hearse all the way, checked out the hole and the vault. He talked and hugged people for reassurance throughout the prayers, but no one objected. Afterwards, we all went to a restaurant for lunch and John ate heartily and with infectious good humor showed snapshots of "my friend Bill boy." He celebrated Bill's life and friendship, rejoiced aloud over many memories represented in the pictures.

John did well. His concept of death is still pretty limited, but we gave him space and a place for saying goodbye, for closure and a happy memory of that day. The ISP staff and I are learning ways to help these clients. They are not children though at times their response is childlike. They have experienced too many years of poor counseling, living through situations in which grieving was denied, and enduring misguided if well intentioned theology. When the communication skills are limited, it is very difficult to get through all that history and we are just learning how to do this with other means (the hospital visits, the photos, the hugs, the tears, the acceptance of touching the body and rearranging the rosary).

We still have a long way to go. We need to cope with our own mortality so we are freed to avoid some of the terrible mistakes that were made with Bill. We need to learn about the emotional, psychosocial and spiritual aspects of death if we are going to be competent and caring counselors for our elderly mentally retarded. This is a special segment of our aging population, but it is a growing one. We have learned not to brush aside their needs for housing, employment and recreation. We must recognize that there is real grief for many losses—not only death—and good grief openly acknowledged and understood means future wellness. We need to share our expertise. The oncologist needs to help us understand symptoms, the family member or caregiver to provide history and pictures, the staff to help with communication clues and counselors to open all the processes of grieving for our understanding. Only then will our joint efforts produce the mental health which is our goal.

Confronting the National Security State: Ex-NSA Agent, Wife Tell of Ordeal

Interview of Margie and John Gilbert
by Robert L. DeWitt and Mary Lou Suhor

Robert L. DeWitt: Can you expand on how you began to question your role with the National Security Agency, John?

John: Two things were going on parallel in time—the intensity of the Vietnam war, rising public consciousness about what was happening, demonstrations—and my deeper involvement and increased responsibility in the NSA. I was caught in a schizophrenic situation because I had uneasy feelings about many government policies. Margie and I would sit at home and talk about what was happening in the war, the lying, the whole works. And I would have one set of opinions about that.

Then I'd go to work and a magic button would push and say, "O.K., you're at the office now. You don't talk about what you're doing, this is a secure area." I would become a different person. Suddenly now I am dynamic office manager and I'm doing all kinds of clever things and people are listening to me.

Margie: And I wasn't. When John would tell me that his work was fun. I could never understand it, because all I could see were the consequences.

RLD: What was it that captivated you about working in intelligence?

John: I was always trying to uncover pure facts, digging to find answers. Then I would give those answers to the people who make government policies and they would act on the information, supposedly. My job was to make that information as clean and accurate and unbiased as possible.

RLD: You said policy makers would act on your information, supposedly?

John: I remember a high level briefing with several representatives of Joint Chiefs of Staff at the Pentagon. I gave a detailed report on how the Soviet Union planned to fight a war in Central Europe, if it should happen, based on war games they had played over a period of time. When you looked at the material dispassionately you could see their whole strategy was based on defense. They expected NATO to attack them and they had plans to counteract. This had been so consistently a part of their military exercises that it couldn't possibly be a sham to throw the West off track, because their forces were trained to react along defensive lines.

When I finished, two of the guys got up and said, "See, Charlie, I told you those Russians are getting ready to attack. Sure, they make it look defensive but you can also turn around and make it offensive just as easy. Charlie, we've got to watch it." And out the door they went. That may have a certain contemporary ring to it. That's when I started thinking I ought to get out of the system.

Mary Lou Suhor: Margie, what did you mean when you said you weren't listening to John?

Margie: Well, at first we were at odds. I kept trying to drag him to meetings and demonstrations where I was hearing things that made me question our policies in Vietnam, and sometimes John wouldn't agree with me. It was only when we went to hear Dan and Phil Berrigan that we both started coming closer together on our questioning. The Berrigans and Thomas Merton were my life raft in those times. We've just seen the movie "Platoon." That seems closer to the Vietnam experience than the propaganda the government was disseminating. One of its themes is that we Americans have to look at our dark side and accept it, forgive ourselves and each other and move on. Otherwise, we'll repeat the war again in Central America.

MLS: John, you used the word "schizo" to describe how you were torn over your role with the NSA. As I recall, the Berrigans were also worried about the mental health of the policy makers you gave your information to, whom they feared were paranoid or xenophobic. Would you comment?

John: Yeah, it seems ridiculous to say all those guys are crazy, but. . . .

Margie: Not anymore!

John: In all seriousness. I think there is a psychology that builds up in that closed, cloistered military world. It's the officers club and headquarters and their own quarters—that's about the extent of their social life and exposure to the world. They go from one military base to another on the opposite side of the world but they meet the same people. They might get away for a year or two, then through reassignment they're linked up again. They talk to each other, reinforcing their own opinions. I think under those conditions it really is possible for a type of mental illness to develop. Instead of functioning rationally and relating to the world as it really exists, they relate on a set of artificial terms of their own manufacture and that's living in a fantasy world. The danger, of course, is that their actions in that fantasy world can obliterate the real world.

RLD: Did you think the peace demonstrations were effective during the Vietnam War?

John: In the beginning I was skeptical that they could have any impact on national policy. But when Johnson decided not to run again, it became clear that the Administration was listening. I was also reluctant to go to demonstrations because of the effect it might have on my clearance status.

RLD: They were taking a lot of photographs out there.

John: Oh, yes. And that wasn't a foolish consideration because when I came up for clearance renewal I had to fill out a personal history. When it was time for the interview and the lie detector test the security guys were primed for me. They accused me of having radical publications in my house. Over past years we had subscribed to *Newsweek*, and suddenly *Newsweek* wasn't on the list any more. Instead, it's CALC's *American Report* and *Post American* and other things.

Then they asked me what demonstrations my wife and I had attended. There was a lot of tooth-sucking going on by those two guys, with nobody smiling much. This went on for two and a half hours one Friday afternoon, and as I drove home I was thinking, was there anything I forgot to include? That's the kiss of death, to hide anything? When I got home I told Margie which demonstrations I had reported. She said I didn't go to that one. I went to this other one, and that one, and I had made a hash of it.

MLS: Margie, how were you reacting to this?

Margie: I was angry they were even questioning what we were doing, and then I became frightened because I wondered where they were getting that information. They must have been checking the mail or phones. Both of us agonized over that weekend.

John: It was the most miserable couple of days in my life. I was worried I had given them false information, unwittingly, and was I in trouble. We sat down and tried to sort it out. Then I thought, this is still a sort-of-free country. This is crazy! So the next morning I told them I had mistakenly given them wrong information and my wife and I had made a correct list. "But damned if I'm going to give it to you," I said, and put it back in my pocket. "It's none of your business. All you have to worry about is whether I'm selling or giving away secrets, and I'm not doing that. You guys have a sticky job, especially since Ellsberg released the Pentagon papers, but you either have to take my word that I'm not giving away secrets or fire me." Then I got written up and put into security files.

RLD: Did you find that out through the Freedom of Information Act?

John: Not through the FOIA. A separate act covers government employees. When I inquired, this guy gives me a big pile of stuff but says, "I have to tell you that certain documents have been taken out, and all I can say is who controls them and the dates." I ended up with two pages of documents which had been removed by the Navy Department, the Army, a whole bunch of investigative organizations, all various dates, and obviously some of them dealt with attendance at demonstrations.

MLS: Were there files on you, too, Margie?

Margie: I wrote to the NSA but they said they didn't have anything, so I didn't pursue it. But what I did write for was transcripts from the Congressional hearings about government infiltrations into groups like Clergy and Laity, the American Friends Service Committee, and other peace groups which had been spied upon even though they were conducting perfectly legal activities. Have you ever seen it? It's inches thick.

RLD: In retrospect, would you say that in your case the system worked? The procedures in screening and surveillance?

John: That's right. I'm not working for them anymore. And I was careful to burn all my bridges behind me so even if I wanted to, there would be no way I could ever go back. But another aspect of it was although I could look at my security file and see I was a "bad guy" in their terms, when I looked at my personnel file which dealt with how I did my job, the two seemed to be about different people. I consistently got outstanding performance ratings and early promotions.

But the whole thing kept building in my conscience. I still have that picture of Oppenheimer. He was the key man in building the atomic bomb and he ended up saying, "What have I done? I've created a monster!" I was getting that feeling. The everyday work was fun, the task of analysis and organization and discovery. It was like doing a crossword puzzle. But the significance hit when I went to my other life. On my way home, the moral judgments began to bother me about what I was doing. It was as though I was trying to serve two masters.

RLD: Let me change the subject a bit. Margie, you wrote The Witness *that there was a sense of conflict between things about your native culture, the United States, and those where you were temporarily residing. Could you elaborate? What kind of attraction in German or English culture did you feel was running athwart of what you were about? When John was studying Russian war games what were you doing?*

Margie: Well, John couldn't tell me anything about the work, whether we were here or overseas. But early on I became curious about Russian culture. I began reading their famous authors, including some of Karl Marx and Lenin. Then I turned to music. I became fascinated with the beauty of their culture, and began to see the Russian people as human beings. I couldn't feel towards them as an enemy. Then I started studying Chinese. I took a course at Catholic University on Chinese philosophy. We later asked the teacher if he would teach us the language. I kept thinking how much better it would be if we were exposed to different languages and music and literature. It's so senseless to be fighting over our little boundaries, saying we're better than you are.

And living overseas gives you a different perspective of what's happening in your own country. Just being exposed to British news media was interesting because they had fewer axes to grind in reporting about Vietnam. Some of the Americans there were angry. They thought the British media were biased in reporting the war.

MLS: You also wrote that it was difficult to be in touch with your friends abroad. Why was that?

Margie: When we were in Germany our landlady's daughter used to babysit for us, and we became good friends. She could speak English and I wrote to her and our landlady too after we got back. They called John into Security and suggested we stop corresponding.

John: I told them my wife was the letter writer, that our babysitter had married and sent pictures of her husband; it was on that level. They said, "Well we can't make your wife stop corresponding with them, but we can make you wish that she did."

MLS: Have you read James Bamford's book about the NSA, The Puzzle Palace? *The book indicates that it's such a secret operation that NSA means No Such Agency.*

John: I read it with great interest because it mentions some of my contemporaries, but it doesn't come across with the exciting aspects of NSA—what attracts people to work there. Quite clearly he tapped into people who knew the agency well, many of the descriptions are what I remember. But he also might have been consciously spoon-fed information to present a picture that things aren't as bad as they seem, to diffuse the problems.

MLS: What about the book's description of civilian and military struggle for control?

John: There was for a number of years civilian/military conflict about who would dominate, but now, to a large extent, civilians are working harmoniously alongside the military. There will always be a certain tug-of-war because the military believes that martial things are incomprehensible to civilians because they haven't been to West Point, which is sheer rubbish. But the military and civilian elements in NSA and the Pentagon have buried the hatchet. They have found that cooperation helps them to achieve higher levels—in budget and overall goals. That merger is frightening.

Eisenhower used to talk about the military-industrial complex, but now there is no separation between the two. What drives the two together to a great extent is the size of contracts.

MLS: Are you referring to the so-called "revolving door" between them?

John: Right. Civilians in the government and military officials administer the contracts and upon retirement they step into a

$100,000 a year job in industry because they have the contacts in government and the Pentagon. And civilians have moved from NSA to the industrial side and back again. The revolving door works constantly.

RLD: You have no fear of saying these things publicly now?

John: Well, I think we've both reached the point where, to a large extent, we don't care. Our convictions have become stronger.

Margie: The fear is gone and a sense of humor has come back.

John: Today there seem to be many people questioning the system. Things are challenged routinely now that would never have been dreamt of, say, 25 years ago or in the McCarthy era. People can understand better what's happening in El Salvador and they spot the softness in an alibi, as when General Haig said, "Maybe those nuns were running a roadblock, and that's why they got shot." Some years ago, people might have bought that, but now it's seen as ridiculous. I think that's very promising.

Margie: Looking at recent events, it seems as though the government has not changed. Our leaders are still playing 'gate' games. Watergate, Contragate, Irangate. But I see hope in people-to-people exchanges. Here in Maine Samantha Smith's visit to Russia was a poignant time for us. How refreshing to see the Russian people through the eyes of a child! There are now plans for an exchange program between University of Maine students and Russian students. And I attended a seminar in September sponsored by Physicians for Social Responsibility where I heard Soviet scientists and doctors who had treated the victims of Chernobyl share their experience. Ironically, another speaker on the program was Admiral Noel Gayler, former director of the NSA.

RLD: What is your denominational background?

John: We were brought up Catholic in Milwaukee. We were high school sweethearts.

Margie: We were influenced by the Young Christian Workers movement, in which you applied the Gospel and principles you were studying to daily work.

MLS: Where do you get your courage to speak out?

Margie: I love reading the Gospels, ever since I was a child while I used to read them during Mass when I became bored. That's pretty much where I center all my thoughts and feelings.

John: Most of my strength comes from Margie. I'm not saying that to flatter her. She seems to delve more into things. She'll be vacuuming and come talk to me about something she was thinking about. When I'm out there tuning up the car, I'm not thinking about El Salvador or nuclear weapons. Or when I'm working in the garden, I'm thinking about putting in seeds, pulling weeds, not about where this world's going.

I have to admit I probably would have continued in the NSA for a long time. The pay was good. I was virtually assured of continuous promotions, there were lots of perquisites. It was a tremendous relief after having had to struggle with family budgeting and keeping little envelopes with totals written on them about how much we had for what. With NSA if I wanted to buy something I simply laid down dollar bills.

RLD: Where do you work now?

John: At the woolen mill. I work as director of personnel. I've also been a bobbin stripper, a weaver, a percher, a lab technician and a dyer.

Margie: Several of us have worked in the mill at one time or another. I was spinning, our son was weighing yarn.

John: For a while we were back to those little envelopes, but now the future seems a little brighter, economically. In a way, talking about leaving the NSA is like watching old home movies. Looking back, it pales in comparison to some of the things we've been through since. It might sound like a dramatic decision to some, but for us it was only an inevitable step on a path of growth.

Hazardous Waste and Holy Ground

by John Finn

God's invitation to action is evident in some extraordinary places. Even hazardous waste dumps.

One bright fall afternoon, I visited a site which had been a bustling plant, but was now a vast expanse of dusty grassland and railroad ties. As I walked down a steep path, I caught a glimpse of the shimmering river which borders the site. Willows leaned over the riverbank and the opposite bank was a leafy rainbow of colors. I reached the river's edge and saw to my horror small globs of black tar oozing out from the bank and sinking down into the river bottom. There was an oily sheen on the surface.

Through the clear water I could see the tar globs which had collected, some as large as a basketball. I felt a pit in my stomach and said, "This simply should not be!" Neglect and ignorance had led to a tragic situation which was clearly a threat to Creation.

In moments like this, God's call sounds more like a shout than a subtle beckoning. To me, waste dumps like this represent sin: sin born of greed, ignorance, and uncaring. I believe that Christians are called to respond to such brokenness, and care for the earth. In my work as an environmental engineer trying to find and clean up hazardous waste dumps, I try to hear this call.

Often the problems needing attention are not so easily discovered. The truth must be painstakingly uncovered. Site investigations are an aspect of my work that could be considered a ministry of ardently pursuing the truth.

Last year, I investigated a sugar refinery. By speaking with ten employees, walking over the entire site, and finally tracing the flow from one particular pipe, I found an innocent-looking ditch. I suspected a dilute lead solution had flowed into that ditch for many years. Sure enough, a careful sampling showed that the soil was laden with high levels of accumulated lead. The ditch is now being

cleaned up, but the sin had to be revealed before that small part of
the earth could be healed.

The activity of actually cleaning up such a problem is the most
rewarding part of my work. Compassion demands action. I most
clearly see my work as a ministry when I can help bring healing to
those festering wounds which threaten the soil, water, and air that
make life possible.

Currently I'm working on several projects where oily pollutants
have contaminated the soil over large areas. Instead of hauling this
soil over hundreds of miles to a "secured landfill" to be stockpiled,
I work on ways to safely biodegrade the pollutants into their harm-
less components. This is done by simply enhancing the earth's
amazing ability to heal itself.

Another aspect of ministry in my work has to do with risks. The
call to any ministry is also a call to the Cross, a call to accept the
inevitable risks involved. My work with hazardous waste is no different. Certainly, significant efforts are made to minimize the risk of
exposure to the very chemicals I am trying to investigate and clean
up. The policy is to wear the protective gear appropriate for the
dangers involved. But there is always "risk" of the unknown.

I once used the standard protection of gloves and goggles to
take soil samples outside of a plant where a previous study suggested slight contamination by crank-case oil and gasoline from trucks.
Months later, a nearby transformer was discovered to have leaked
hazardous PCBs in the same area. If I had known, I would have
worn two pairs of gloves, boots, coveralls, and a full-face respirator.

Naturally, we anticipate situations like this as best we can. There
are risks, though, and in order to do this work at all, I need to
accept them.

Of course, there are restrictions which prevent my ministry from
being exercised to its fullest. I work for a private company and one
of the most serious restrictions is the constant concern for the cost
in dollars. On the days when I spend most of my time making sure
the company is making a profit, I begin to wonder where my ministry has gone.

Often the budget I have for a project is inadequate for the work
which should be done. I recently helped investigate the environmental status of some fifty manufacturing plants. The best way to do
this is to actually visit the plants and inspect them. Even then, it is
difficult to determine what may lie beneath the surface. But our
client only had enough money for us to ask questions over the telephone. That's frustrating, because I know a lot was not being
revealed. Similarly, the clean-ups we recommend are often rejected
or postponed because they are "too expensive."

Another frustration is that the problems seem so much larger than what I do to help solve them. Every workday I hear about three or four newly discovered hazardous waste sites all over the country. Yet work on the few we know about proceeds at a painfully slow pace. I groan with the earth for the New Creation. I often need to hear the children in my neighborhood laugh and play or hike along a path in the woods to remember how God intends things to be.

In these moments of reflection, I am thankful for God's invitation to care. In my work I seek to respond to that invitation by revealing the sins of hazardous waste dumping and taking action to heal them. Someday I may be called to serve in a different way. But for now, when I remember that black tar oozing down into the river, I realize that this is an important ministry.

Lay Ministry Battle Story

by Emma Lou Benignus

A woman research technician on the staff of a hospital was asked by the surgeon to call on a young man deprived by extensive surgery of the use of both legs and all functions in the lower part of his body. He preferred to die and probably would. What bothered him and caused self-rejection and severe depression was not death but the loss of his manhood. The ignominy of his situation pierced his soul. His doctor asked the technician to visit him, to relate to him, to "talk with him as a woman to a man." In addition to all of his other woes, the young man was fighting gangrenous peritonitis and the accompanying odor at times was horrendous.

As the technician entered his room, she gagged, quickly backed out the door, and fled down the hall, only to run into the doctor. "Have you seen my young man?" he asked, his eyes alight with hope. "I tried, but I couldn't breathe," she said. With much kindness and with firm grip on her arm, the surgeon turned her again toward the patient's room, walked with her, and admitted, "I know it smells bad, but there is a man in there, a heartbroken young man. You are a woman. Please go to him and find the man inside that stink." With that he opened the door and steered her through.

The surgeon's great caring heart all that week summoned her to acts of self-transcendence through which the sick man eventually was reached and was comforted before he died.

Three years later, when the technician was meditating on the Incarnation, from nowhere came recollection of the doctor's words. A wave of recognition overwhelmed her; she knew that she herself was as that man, and that God had sent his Son into the world not only to find him but to find her and others like her "inside the human stink." Such is the work of the laity—to recognize the presence of God in the affairs of the world, and in whatever way possible, to embody, to incarnate, that Presence.

Is This Ministry?

by Nell Braxton Gibson

I am a black woman, a wife, mother, homemaker. I have fought for
human rights all my life. I volunteer my time as a member of the
Board of Theological Education, the Episcopal Commission of Black
Ministries and the Berkeley Board of Trustees at Yale Divinity
School. I have been a vestry member, Sunday School teacher, parish
secretary, Girls Friendly Society leader and camp counselor. I have
counseled and taught seminary students and I have done hard physical labor building classrooms and a chapel in the African bush of
Tanzania. I've tested Fair Housing Laws in California, registered
black voters, picketed and been jailed in Georgia. I grew up in the
South and spent my formative years living in Mississippi.

I am a Christian.

Sometimes when people (who know I don't work at a paid nine
to five job) ask me what I do, I tell them I am an unordained minister. They don't always believe me. Maybe it's because I don't always
believe myself. Ministry is a difficult business which can leave one
with many self doubts and feelings of inadequacy. Lay ministry is
harder in many ways than ordained because it isn't always recognized.

There are times when no one asks me what I do and times
when I go about the business of living without much thought of
God or ministry. Like the day I left my sick 10-year-old son home
alone so I could attend a meeting. I promised I'd return as soon as
I could and bring him a special hamburger lunch treat. But I ran
into a friend on my way home and she was in tears, so I called
home, explained why I'd be late and bought *her* lunch. She told me
her ex-husband was late with the child support payment, her lover
was leaving her for another woman, there was an eviction notice on
her front door and her children needed shoes. We talked of many
things that day—our families, our responsibilities, our aging parents, our getting older. Toward the end of lunch we found our-

selves singing the praises of black women; women who have supported their men, nurtured their children—just hung in there and
survived. We talked about the burden laid on us always to be
strong, and how hard it was to live up to that image. We acknowledged that there are times when we want to be taken care of, held,
loved and understood. We admitted to having cried during these
times and then come out on top again, stronger and more determined than ever. I left her feeling a new surge of life.

I took Bert III his special hamburger treat, then played backgam-
mon with him. When eight-year-old Erika came home from school I
drove her to track practice and worked on a book I am writing
while she and her teammates got ready for the Colgate Women's
Games. After track practice I drove several of the girls home and
picked up my husband's suit at the cleaners for his forthcoming
business trip. Then I went home to prepare dinner, stopping to
help Erika with homework. I gave young Bert another dose of med-
icine and ironed a week's supply of shirts for Bert's trip. Within
minutes he came through the front door dejected and tired. He is
Financial Vice-President of a non-profit organization and that day
he'd discovered his projected budget was $1 million over. His staff
had to work overtime and he was going to have to work during the
weekend. His boss was out of town and he would have to call her
to break the news. After unleashing all his angry feelings, he turned
to me accusingly and asked if I had forgotten to pick up his suit. I
put my arms around him, told him I hadn't forgotten and suggested
he change his clothes while I made two gin and tonics and played
our favorite Chuck Mangione album.

I don't know a great deal about balancing budgets but I do
know what administrative changes might help prevent a situation
like that from recurring, so I suggested some. He agreed and by the
end of the evening he had figured how to cut the deficit in half. He
felt that with a good night's sleep he'd probably be able to present
to the Board figures close to his originally projected budget.

Several days later I was off to the mountains with the ISTEM
seminary students for a retreat. I led a group exercise on racism
which proved devastating to the black and Hispanic students
because of the attitudes expressed by many of their white colleagues. Heated discussions and verbal attacks left everyone upset.
We came together after dinner again to wrestle with the problems.
We ended the night with prayer but without having resolved the
issues. Several of us poured drinks, others played ping pong, went
for walks or sat around and talked. The other black staff member
and I asked a couple of students to join us in a game of bid whist.
In the middle of the game a black male student used the word,

"priestess" to describe one of the female students. Tempers were still running high, and she lashed out at him calling him a "closet sexist." He became defensive and verbally fought back—yelling about what society had done to him as a black man and of all seminary had done to him by demanding an education which alienated him from his own people. He talked about the white minister he worked for who was continually saying he was aggressive, impatient, arrogant, and too anxious to express the black point of view. Tears welled in his eyes when he told how he had tried to commit suicide two years before. As he talked I took both his hands in mine and when he had finished I said, "I've been there." He was astonished! I told him I'd felt the same pain, known the same hurt, cried the same tears for all the same reasons. I had lived through it and he would too.

A few months later I found myself at a Board meeting asking whether or not the accounting firm we had chosen had any blacks or women working as accountants, whether our donors were also supporting apartheid in South Africa, and why there were so few blacks entering seminary. At another Board meeting a priest whom I love and care about got up and walked out in the middle of a report. I worried about him all the way home. When I had a few minutes I called to ask if everything was all right. He told me he'd been going through a painful divorce and was feeling low. He was the second priest I'd talked with in less than a year who was struggling through a divorce. I let both of them know of my deep concern, and told each I'd be praying for him.

In a book called *Monday's Ministries*, Nelvin Vos says that ministry is performed in the struggles of human life; that those struggles include:

> "Living with a hassle
> Caring, no matter what the cost
> Responding, with no strings attached
> Seeing others' needs
> Being vulnerable
> Being open
> Perceiving suffering
> Responding nonverbally"

Our tradition as blacks is to "tell the story." That is why I find illustrations better than any other means of sharing my ministry. I know Christ works through me, healing my brokenness as he helps me heal others. I know I am sustained through prayers as God helps me comfort and support others through prayer. I know I need the love and support of those around me in order to carry out my ministry and that support and love come from the people I serve most—my family and friends.

Two weeks after I underwent major surgery, the friend I took to lunch came to clean my home. She also cooked dinner for my family and kept me company while her own children ate at their home alone. She said she did it because she did not have money to buy me flowers or candy. My daughter, who taught me "The Rock" and "Patty Duke," urged me to swallow my pride at her father's office party and get out on the dance floor to show them what she had taught me. She reminded me that I'm always telling her she must overcome her shyness and that I had to overcome mine too. My son took me to Central Park and helped me field baseballs so that I wouldn't be embarrassed by missing easy pop-ups when I pitched for his Saturday ball game. My husband leaves love notes pinned to my pillow when he goes away on trips, reaches out to me with understanding when I am discouraged and strongly supports my independence by encouraging me to be my own person, do my own thing, live my life fully. That is how they minister to me.

The true meaning of ministry is service. The meaning of *laos* is people. I am a lay minister because I am one of the people who serves.

Ministry in the Marketplace

by William E. Diehl

"Mr. Diehl, how can you possibly say you are a Christian and yet continue to work, as an executive, for a large corporation in the business field?" That question has been put to me directly by more than one student as I have lectured on seminary campuses. It has been implied by many others in the religious community through other questions they have asked.

Can a Christian be in business today? More than that, can there be Christian ministry in the marketplace? The student's question is a troubling one because it suggests a distorted notion of the world and a misunderstanding of some basic Christian doctrine.

While critics of the world of business can point to the detrimental consequences of competition, materialism, and selfishness, the marketplace has no lock on the evils of human nature. I have seen vicious competition on college campuses among both students and faculty. The lust for power and prestige is common in government and politics, as well as in business. Materialism is typical of the lifestyle of top performers in the fields of entertainment and sports. Selfish people are liberally sprinkled through all segments of U.S. society. There are many aspects of business that do indeed need to be improved or changed, but to suggest that business is the field that brings out the worst of human nature is to demonstrate a distorted understanding of our culture.

The student's question, also, demonstrates some ideas of Christian doctrine that differ substantially from my own. It has been my understanding that "The earth is the Lord's and the fullness thereof, the world and they that dwell therein." When we read in Genesis that "God saw all that he had made, and it was very good," do we add "except for those parts of creation which we judge to be evil"? Has God given up on certain parts of his creation, or does he still love and care about all of it? When we read that "God so loved the world, that he gave his only begotten Son," do we exclude the world of business?

One also has to ask about the doctrine of salvation. To suggest that one's occupation validates or denies one's Christian status is to define Christianity on the basis of what we do rather than who we are. In baptism we were brought into the family of God. We do not say that the relationship is taken away, based on one's later occupation. Paul reminds us that we are justified by faith alone, apart from what we do. In the same manner that there is no such thing as a Christian field goal in football or a Christian appendectomy in a hospital, there is no such thing as a Christian business deal. Yes, field goals can be kicked by Christians, and appendectomies can be performed by Christians, and business deals can be negotiated by Christians, but it is neither the football field nor the operating room nor the marketplace that defines whether or not the participant is a Christian. They are neutral grounds. It is the relationship that the football player or the surgeon or the businessman has with the Creator, through baptism into the Christian family, that defines his or her status.

Throughout the Old Testament and New Testament, we read that all the people of God are members of a royal priesthood. As priests, we are the channels of God's love for his creation. The whole incarnational principle indicates that God's action in the world comes through human beings. There is absolutely no suggestion in our Scriptures that certain parts of creation are "off limits" for God's love and concern. Therefore, as priests of our Lord, we do not absent ourselves from segments of society. Jesus ministered among the social and political outcasts of his time; he drew the line at no one. Should we do any less?

Can there be Christian ministry in the marketplace? There must be Christian ministry in the marketplace! I have come to see a variety of ministries that are necessary in the marketplace. Here they are:

The Ministry of Competency

St. Augustine put it very well. When asked why he bought his sandals from a non-Christian craftsman instead of another who was a Christian, he replied, "Because he makes better sandals, and I do too much walking to put up with inferior sandals." We live in an extremely complex society. We depend upon the work of so many people to make our society function well. To the degree that people do their jobs well, they minister to all of us. We depend upon airline pilots to get us safely to a destination. Judy and I have four children, who have been placed in the hands of scores of school-teachers. To the degree to which they did a good job of teaching our dear children, they ministered to us. As we carry out our jobs to the best of our ability and to the glory of God, we minister to one another.

Even a salesperson? Yes, even a salesperson. Early in my career with Bethlehem Steel, I was assigned to our Detroit sales office. My job was to sell construction products, which were fabricated in a shop outside the city. It became apparent to me very early that the workers in that shop were depending on me to do a good job of selling. Every time my car pulled into the parking lot of the shop, the foreman would come out to see if I had secured a new construction products' contract. When I brought in orders, the men in the shop were certain of work. It was obvious that entire families were counting upon me to provide for their basic necessities. Later, as a sales manager, I became very impatient with any of our salespeople who began coasting because they didn't plan to go any farther in the company. "Listen," I'd say, "maybe you don't care, but the people in those steel plants care! they are counting on us to provide work for them, and we are going to do our best!"

Managers and supervisors have a special calling for competency. It is they who teach, coach, encouage, and support their people so that all perform to the best of their ability. In a world in which most people have never fully developed their human potential, the manager has a sacred responsibility: To help people grow to their fullest capabilities. As a management consultant, I have found it extremely ironic that those organizations that are in the "phone business"—social-service agencies and church organizations—disdain the very notion of using good management skills and, thereby, hurt their own staffs. Most for-profit organizations know that the farther down the ladder they can delegate responsibility and decision making, the more efficiently they operate. The for-profits work at developing human potential; most of the nonprofits do not. It's tragic.

The ministry of competency is the first level of Christian ministry—in the marketplace or elsewhere.

The Ministry of Interpersonal Relationships

A job in the marketplace almost always involves person-to-person relationships with many people. There are customers, suppliers, coworkers, support staff, and owners or managers. The fact is that during our working years we spend more hours of the day in relationship with people in our place of work than with our own families. The quality of those relationships can define our ministry.

Most of us are poor listeners to begin with. In the workplace, we tend to be so much consumed by our own tasks that alertness to the personal messages sent out by our associates is even further diminished. It is entirely possible for one to work side by side with another human being for years and never really know that person. We can interact with an associate all day in the workplace without ever picking up a clue that he or she is hurting. Why is this so? It is primarily that we are not intentional about developing open relationships with others and improving our interpersonal skills, like being a good listener.

At Bethlehem Steel, we gave all our young salespeople a course in effective listening. We worked hard at improving their interpersonal relationships, especially with regard to being a good listener. Many a sale has been lost because the salesperson failed to pick up the message that was being conveyed in the midst of many words. In the same way that we need to concentrate on effective listening at the point of sale, we need to be just as intentional in our listening to all our associates in the work place. This, too, is ministry.

The ministry of interpersonal relationships also suggests that we need to be very sensitive to cultural and ethnic differences in the workplace. This awareness should govern our interaction with others, but it also provides an opportunity for more than that. Much of our prejudice toward others is thoughtless and results from impressions made upon us long ago. When people of good will are given an occasion to look at their own thoughtlessness, most will become more sensitive to cultural and ethnic differences among their associates. So, we have a teaching ministry to perform.

For some persons, the work place relationships that are developed become their "family." This is not to suggest that the job should replace one's family in the order of priorities. We already have too many workaholics who have neglected their families with tragic consequences. But there are some persons who literally have no natural family, or at least none in close enough proximity to provide the nurturing function of family. For these persons the job is the center of their lives, and the work place associates become family. We can minister to these persons by being aware of their needs and by providing support for them. In fact, to include them as part of one's extended family and to invite them for special family events, such as Thanksgiving dinner or a Memorial Day picnic, may be an appropriate and effective way to minister to their needs. The ministry of interpersonal relationships has within it a wide range of possbilities.

The Ministry of Stewardship

In many jobs in the marketplace we are called upon to be good stewards of the resources of another. A sales clerk is steward of the merchandise he or she has available for sale. An office worker is entrusted with computer equipment, copy machines, communication equipment, and other tools to accomplish the job. Obviously, we are expected to be honest and careful in our use of these resources. In some companies, workers are permitted a "reasonable" use of copy machines or telephones for personal needs. In such instances, good judgment is necessary. Furthermore, we are able to be good stewards of our use of time. If we are expected to give eight hours of work, that's what it should be.

Perhaps all the above is so obvious that it didn't need saying. What doesn't seem to be so obvious, however, is that the principle of good stewardship applies at all levels of the business organization. There is reason to be critical of many people in management who somehow assume that the higher they go in the organization, the more freedom they have to use the company's resources in their own interests.

Expense accounts are the most obvious examples. Many managers use company expense accounts to cover trips, entertainment, or meals that really do not contribute to the benefit of the organization. And such use is not considered cheating. We call such advantages "perks." They are part of the way we do business. Everybody does business that way. If I'm a sales manager and my competition is entertaining customers, I had better do the same. I may just happen to select those customers whose likes are similar to mine—golf, theater, gourmet dining, or whatever. But why not? It comes with the job.

When one visits the corporate offices of some of our major business and law firms, one has to question the practice of stewardship. Huge amounts of company resources have gone into the furnishing of executive offices. Expensive desks, rich carpeting and draperies, antique furniture, exquisite art, private bathrooms with stall showers—these are the marks of success in business. If a new executive moves into an office, it is refurnished to his or her taste, no matter how recently it has been decorated before. It really is a shameful waste of corporate resources. Perhaps the law firms are worse.

Presumably the corporate jets and the company limousines conserve the time of busy executives; in many instances that is true. But, all too easily, the limos can be used for personal trips, and the company jets make an extra stop at an airport to accommodate an executive and spouse who ask to "hitch a ride."

Must there be separate corporate dining facilities for the high-brow, middle-brow and low-brow employees? If the secretaries manage to negotiate cafeteria lines, why must the top brass have special table service around huge, walnut tables in paneled rooms? It can't be to save time; the managers have oodles of time to talk about golf, football, and the stock market. Somehow, the Japanese have managed to do pretty well by integrating their lunch facilities. It's curious how the top brass learns more about the company when they eat lunch with the workers.

The point is that those who would minister in the marketplace need to consider the matter of stewardship throughout the organization, and they should be especially sensitive to the abuse of resources as they move into management.

There is another issue of stewardship that primarily relates to management. It has to do with short-term performance. Wall Street closely monitors reports of earnings. A dip in one corporation's quarterly earnings can send the price of its stock down, while glowing returns from another company will frequently boost its stock value. As a result, there is great pressure within American corporations to do that which will have an immediate impact on corporate earnings, even at the expense of long-term profitability. The annual bonuses of many managers are directly related to the price of the company's stock. So within many corporations, projects that might have a beneficial long-term result are scrapped in favor of those that provide a quick profit. It takes a manager of great courage to argue for long-term strategies when all the rest of the organization is intent on quick results. Yet, in the overall interests of the organization, the long-term projects can often be the best stewardship of corporate resources.

The biblical concept of stewardship—of caring for that which has been entrusted to us—has numerous applications in the marketplace. It is a vital piece of Christian ministry.

The Ministry of Ethical Decision Making

On Decemger 3, 1984, a tragic accident at the Union Carbide Plant in Bhopal, India, took the lives of 1,700 people and injured an additional 200,000. Much has been written about the cause of the accident and what steps might have averted it. But nowhere in the stories has there been any suggestion that the accident was the result of a premeditated act of top management. It was an accident. Yet, all admit that it was an accident that didn't need to have happened. Something went wrong in the system. Those of us who have worked in large organizations know only too well that actions taken by persons of the highest moral character can turn out to be tragic. Why?

For one thing, we need to recognize that we work in institutions that take on lives of their own. The character and style of a corporation is not simply the sum total of the character and styles of those who work in it at any given time. Corporate culture is developed over long periods of time and is frequently difficult to change in the short run, as many a new CEO (Chief Executive Officer) has found. William Stringfellow suggested that the institutions of our society indeed become demonic. They tend to possess those who work for them. Likening them to the "principalities and powers" to which the Apostle Paul makes frequent reference, Stringfellow wrote that the organizations of our society, profit and nonprofit, develop their own existence, personality, and mode of life. Reinhold Niebuhr made a similar assertion in his book *Moral Man and Immoral Society*. If this is true, and I believe it is, then there needs to be more intentional checking of the decision-making process in our corporations.

Most corporations have a manufacturing department, a sales department, an accounting department, a law department, a purchasing department, and many more. But, very few have a department of ethics. Why? Well, we assume that if good, ethical people make decisions, the outcomes will be able to stand up under ethical review. Yet, it didn't happen at Bhopal, India, and it hasn't happened in hundreds of other instances.

A few years ago, while I was still at Bethlehem Steel, we faced a decision about whether or not to close a manufacturing operation which had been losing money for two years. A young accountant assigned to our department was very assertive about why we should shut down the operation. Knowing of the cyclical history of that shop, I was urging a bit more patience. He kept pressing. Finally, in desperation, I said, "Well, what about the people who have worked there for all these years? Don't we owe them a bit more time?" He shot back, "It's not my job to think about the people!" And, he was right. His job was to crunch the numbers, period. Was it my job, as sales manager, to worry about the workers? No such item was in my job description. And I wondered where, in our system, will someone ask that question about our responsibility to the workers?

Until such time as the marketplace does undertake an ethical study of corporate decisions, it seems to me that there is a Christian ministry in raising the awkward question about our decision making. That is risky. To question the morality of decisions made by management is to question the morality of managers. Why? Because

we kid ourselves into thinking that we are in control of our institutions, instead of realizing that frequently they control us.

There have been instances in recent years in which top management ignored or second-guessed warnings about product design
from within the organization. Where this happened and accidents
have occurred, management has to accept the responsibility. But the
problem is that not enough questions or warnings come from within the system. We always assume someone else is taking care of the
ethical implications, because it is "not our job." It is a risky, career-
threatening business, but to raise some questions about the quality
of decisions in the marketplace is, indeed, Christian ministry.

The Ministry of Change

During the 1960s, when the environmental movement was gathering popular support, I would occasionally be challenged with,
"What are *you* doing to clean up the steel industry?" To which I
answered "Nothing!"

Having mentioned in the previous section the need to risk awkward questions about decision making, it must be added that one
has to assess one's potential for bringing about change. The environmental issue is a good example. The steel industry was a dirty
one. It polluted the waters, air, and earth. But during the 1960s the
steel producers were pouring what limited financial resources they
had into new plants and equipment in order to stay competitive.
For any one of them to divert millions of dollars into pollution-control equipment at the expense of new production equipment would
be to give their competitors an advantage. No amount of questions
from environmentally concerned employees would change the situation. Unless every steel producer was required to clean up its
plant, none would do so. What was needed, in this situation, was
legislation requiring all steel companies to install pollution-control
equipment. That's what happened and that's why the steel towns are
much cleaner today.

It is my conviction that the major changes in the marketplace
almost always come as a result of outside pressure or legislation. It
is not reasonable to expect Christians, within the organization, to
effect change on the major issues.

Where there is the potential for a ministry of change in the marketplace, it is with respect to the corporate culture and the treatment of people. The old patterns of sex, race, and age discrimination can be erased within the organization by persons who seek to
bring about change.

After the women in my family succeeded in opening my eyes to sexism in the work place, I decided to try an experiment. I had just been made the manager of the department. Shortly after moving in, I went to the small room where we kept the coffeepot and poured myself a cup of coffee. As I returned to my office, my new secretary said, "Oh, I'll get your coffee for you, Mr. Diehl." I replied that, no, it was OK. I would get my own coffee. The other men in the department soon noticed what I was doing, and one by one they stopped asking the women to bring them their coffee. Before long, everyone was going for his or her coffee and, in time, we even had an assignment sheet posted as to who would make the coffee in the morning. After a while, our department become known as "the one where everybody gets their own coffee." I learned many years later that other departmental managers picked up the idea and, surprise, surprise, the other men in their departments soon followed, also. Some managers may say that my time was too valuable to be wasting it on going for coffee. Baloney! Management time is frittered away on many nonproductive things. Besides, good managers go out where the people are, anyway.

The Ministry of Values

One of the criticisms of the marketplace is that it fosters such values as status, materialism, power, obsession with security, selfishness, and the like. While such values are not found exclusively in the marketplace, they do, indeed, exist there. Since many of these values are self-destructive and hurt others as well, an important Christian ministry in the marketplace is to challenge them and work to change them.

The newly appointed executive who turns down the company policy of redecorating offices, whether or not they need them, is raising the issue of values. Do we need elegant surroundings to give visibility to our status? Is status that important?

When I was assistant manager at Bethlehem Steel my car had an especially designated spot on the second floor of the company garage. I was surprised one morning, shortly after my promotion to manager, to drive into my familiar stall only to find a strange name on it. So, I parked the car outside the garage and called the administrative supervisor to ask what had happened. "Oh, you're now down on the first floor with all the other managers," he explained. "Why must I park with the other managers?" I asked. "Well, it's kind of a status symbol to have a better parking spot," he replied. "I don't want status symbols," I said. "Besides, I like the people I've been parking with. Why must I leave them?" The administrator had a hard time believing I was for real, but after I threatened to leave the garage if I didn't have the old spot back, he agreed. So, I had my own little statement about status. I learned some months later, from my secretary, that the chief engineer in our department, a very status-conscious man, suddenly agreed to let his secretary use his second-floor parking stall when he was out of town. Previously no one else had been permitted to use his "status symbol."

Through our ministry of values, we really are communicating the Gospel of Jesus Christ in contemporary forms. Jesus promised us that we would know the truth and the truth would set us free. The truth is that we are saved by the grace of God alone, without regard to anything we do to merit that gift of grace. Power, prestige, wealth, and status mean nothing in the eyes of God. He accepts us as his children. Yet, so many of us are slaves to a works-righteous culture that says that our identity is based on what we do and our worth is based on how well we do it. We become captives of a system that defines human worth in terms of power and material gain. When Christians challenge the values of that system, they are making a theological statement: The Gospel has freed us from the destructive and demonic philosphy of having to prove our worth.

The homes we live in, the cars we drive, the clothes we wear, the clubs to which we belong say much about our values. This is not to suggest that we should renounce all wealth and power. Since we are called to minister in the marketplace, we do need certain tools to do the job effectively. There is a thread running through our Bible that speaks of a "theology of enough." The Lord provided manna for the Israelites in the wilderness, but they were admonished only to take what was needed for that day. Those who took more than they needed discovered on the next day that it had "bred worms and become foul." Jesus warned about the obsession with wealth and storing for tomorrow that which was not needed for today.

If we follow a theology of enough, then it seems to me that we try to live on the down side of the range of our associates. Our homes, our cars, our clothes are modest, but adequate, for carrying out our Christian calling in the marketplace. By practicing and talking about a life-style of "enough," we are ministering to those who are captives of a demonic philosophy that requires them to prove their worth.

What about the high salaries paid to top executives in the marketplace? Again, it is a matter of stewardship and values. There are a few top leaders in the private sector who have chosen to make a statement of their own by eschewing high compensation. Peter

Drucker, the guru of business management, has suggested that it would be wise for there to be a ratio within an organization between the highest and lowest paid jobs. He has even suggested that the ratio be as low as 1 to 10. That is, if the entry-level job in a corporation pays $12,000 a year, the top position can pay no more than $120,000. I'm sure that suggestion went over like a lead balloon with his readers. His reasons had to do with mobilizing support of the whole organization for greater productivity. But whatever the reason, the issue of how much salary is enough for those in leadership positions is worthy of some examination.

Can there be ministry in the marketplace? Of course! As we fulfill our priestly roles in God's world, we can find ministry in competency, interpersonal relationships, stewardship, ethical decision making, change, and values. There's ministry aplenty for all of us.

William E. Diehl, who retired as manager of sales from Bethlehem Steel, is president of Riverbend Resource Center, a management consulting business in Allentown, PA. He is an active layman in the Lutheran Church in America and was among the founders of LAOS in Ministry.

PART III

Educational Support Systems

How can the institutional church develop educational systems to support the ministry of the laity? What are the questions that need to be addressed? What is the most helpful stance the church can assume? What are some more facilitating images the church can have of itself?

The first group of selections deals with the relationship between the church and the world.

The next considers the theological issues.

The third section offers new challenges for the institution. Some people have been thinking and working on developing new strategies. This section offers a sampling to prime the pump.

Relationship Between the Church and the World

The Alban Institute published a pamphlet by Parker Palmer called Going Public, even in title a provocative suggestion for the hidden life of most congregations. Palmer offers some suggestions as to how the public life might be practiced in the congregation.

In preparation for a workshop on lay ministry the Rev. N. Patrick Murray, director of Christ Church, Little Rock, prepared a paper which addresses that hiddenness and reflects on another possibility for the relationship of the church and the world.

Celia Hahn has used the graphic images of the church as a closed system or the church as an open system. The excerpt from her book spells out the cost of the church as a closed system.

There is much going on outside the stained glass walls. Mark Gibbs talks about some of the questions posed for the institution in "Ministries Outside the Parish."

Barbara Campbell, a lay person, wrestles with the issue.

Practicing the Public Life in the Congregation

by Parker Palmer

If the church is to build a bridge between private and public, it must do so not only through its teaching and preaching, but also through the conduct of congregational life. In fact, the most powerful lessons of all are not sermons or classroom exercises, but the experiences people have in the congregation. How can the church practice the public life internally, giving people a taste of public possibilities and some skill at moving in the public realm?

We will make no progress on that question until we recognize that the church is often seen by its members as an extension of private life rather than a bridge into the public. To turn the congregation toward the public life we must resist the lure of another image—the image of the church as "extended family," a closed circle of "our own kind," a community in which the pluralism and abrasions of the public world can be avoided and evaded. We must see that the church has often succumbed to one of the great enemies of public life, the "cult of intimacy."

Whatever else public life may be, it will never be intimate. Our relations in public can be characterized by interest, respect, appreciation, but never by deep inward knowledge of each other. Public relations are the relations of strangers, in which strangers learn to occupy the same space and share a common commitment despite myriad differences between them. The key to public life is learning to appreciate strangers without having either to reject them or turn them into intimates and friends.

The cult of intimacy denies public life by valuing only those relations in which we know the other deeply and are deeply known. Because such knowledge is risky and, at best, possible with only a few, the quest for intimacy leads us into smaller and smaller circles of "meaningful relations." It cuts us off from the richness given by relations of various durations, intensity, and depth. So long as the church sees itself as a community of intimacy it will be a barrier rather than a bridge to the public life.

But the church has an opportunity to be a bridge by demonstrating that diversity, otherness, strangeness can be contained within the framework of a common faith. No demonstration is more vital if public life is to be renewed. We have retreated from public pluralism into private homogeneity because we lack faith that common commitment can hold diversity together. Deeper still, we perceive that the common commitment has withered, but by withdrawing from public life we abandon the very place where that commitment might be renewed. If we are to return to the public realm, we need to see it at work—this process in which diversity is protected but unity achieved—and the church has a chance to show us.

Impossible, you may say, since the typical congregation in its quest for intimacy has already become homogeneous to an extreme. But I suggest that the homogeneity of the congregation is only apparent, a result of people trying to stifle their diversity for the sake of a dream-wish. If the life of the congregation could be redefined to encourage people to express and experience differences within a context of common commitment, the church would become a training ground for the leadership necessary to renew our public life.

How might this be done? I want to suggest some possibilities in two areas of the congregation's life: making decisions and extending hospitality.

Too often congregations try to minimize points at which decisions must be made since these are points at which conflict is likely to occur. We drift along ignoring decisions that need making or let the pastor or a small "power elite" make them on the side, hoping that "the community" can be spared the pain of encountering its own differences. Of course, such a group is no community, for true community comes more from facing and transcending our diversity than from basking in our commonality.

The problem is that decision-making in the church, when it does happen, is often no less abrasive and divisive than decision-making in the world beyond the church. If the church is to lead people from private into public life, it must find a way of making decisions which does not mute our differences but puts them in the context of a common quest, a way which allows us to assert our version of truth but requires us to listen carefully to other versions as well.

Such a way is the method called consensus. Consensus means that no decision is taken until everyone in the group is willing to go along. Consensus puts off people who have no experience of it, for it sounds time-consuming, laborious, and ultimately impossible. How much easier to debate, count up the votes, and declare a winner! Consensus is not as efficient as voting, to be sure, but consensus drives us to a deeper place in ourselves and our relationships than voting ever can. Where voting calls us to defend our own position and defeat others, consensus calls us to scrutinize our own convictions with care. Where voting results in a majority overpowering a minority, consensus teaches us what it means to be a member of a body which must act together. That is, consensus cultivates the virtues required for public life.

What is it about consensus that helps us deal creatively with conflict? Primarily this: When a group cannot make a decision until everyone is willing to go along, the tenor of discussion is quite different than when the majority can rule. Now, instead of listening for differences between us, instead of looking for points we can rebut, we listen instead for similarities, we look for common ground. When the majority rules we try to sharpen the disagreements between us and line up votes for our side. When decisions are made by consensus we seek a synthesis that brings opposites together. This quest for unity is essential to public life.

But at the same time consensus protects the individual's right to conscience (as must the public life). If even one person has grave doubts about the morality of a course of action, the group operating by consensus cannot move. This may sound like organizational insanity, since all of us have been in voting situations where a few people have remained obstinantly unconvinced of the majority's wisdom. But under consensus the individual who objects must do so on carefully considered grounds. When individuals are given the power which consensus bestows, they tend to filter out their minor differences of opinion and stand against the group only when they must. Consensus not only calls us to listen with care to one another; it also requires that we listen carefully to our own inner truth.

Whether or not a given congregation is ready to conduct an experiment with consensus, the underlying challenge should not be lost. The church must find ways of practicing the public life by allowing its members to explore their differences in a framework of common faith, to learn experientially that diversity and unity are not incompatible, that out of many can come one.

Another way the church can practice public life is by extending hospitality to strangers. By this I do not mean coffee hours designed as recruiting events to sign up new members for the church. We fall into the cult of intimacy when we confuse hospitality with an effort to make the stranger "one of us." The essence of hospitality—and of the public life—is that we let our differences, our strangeness, be as they are, while still acknowledging a unity that lies beneath diversity. Here is how Henri Nouwen defines it:

> Hospitality ... means ... the creation of a free space where the stranger can enter.... Hospitality is not to change people, but to offer them space where change can take place. It is not to bring men and women over to our side, but to offer freedom not disturbed by dividing lines. It is not to lead our neighbor into a corner where there are no alternatives left, but to open a wide spectrum of options for choice and commitment.... It is not a method of making our God and our way into the criteria of happiness, but the opening of an opportunity for others to find their God and their way. The paradox of hospitality is that it wants to create emptiness, not a fearful emptiness, but a friendly emptiness where strangers can enter and discover themselves as created free.... Hospitality is not of the host, but the gift of a chance for the guest to find his (or her) own.   (*Reaching Out*, p. 51)

And how might this be done? The possibilities are limited only by imagination and the willingness to try. For example, I recently spent several days volunteering at a soup kitchen run by a church in one of the poorest parts of New York City. Each day, a simple meal of soup and bread and tea is served to the strangers who come in off the street—men and women whose lives have been wasted by mental illness, alcohol, drugs, poverty; people barely able to survive. Those who come in to eat are not asked to give anything in return, but only to receive a gift of food. But those who serve, as I did those few days, receive a gift as well, a gift of understanding. There I was, standing among people whose neighborhood I seldom enter and who never enter mine, people I would have crossed the street to avoid. And as I did so it came to me that if fear were called for, they should be afraid of me, for I represent and profit by a society which has left them bereft.

In this soup kitchen, this place of hospitality, I was able to see the connections between myself and these strangers. I felt the unity that runs beneath our vast and tragic differences. I was reminded that we are members of one another, members of the public. And I thought how helpful it would be if more churches had outposts like this, not only for the sake of those who are hungry, but for the sake of those whose need is to be reminded of their connections and accountability to the least of these, our brethren.

Another example, of quite a different kind: The church could extend hospitality to strangers by offering to host dialogues between groups in the community who are, or may be, in conflict. I mean groups such as teachers and school boards; teenagers and police; blacks and whites in "changing neighborhoods;" labor and management; "gays" and "straights." Everywhere we look today there are groups lining up against one another, viewing each other with all the fear and hostility that the stranger can evoke. The church might help such groups achieve not intimacy but mutual understanding, the capacity to see each other as members of a public.

Of course, the church can offer hospitable space to strangers only as it provides such space for its own members. If a congregation is suppressing conflict within its own life, it cannot play the role of mediator in the larger community. A congregation must cultivate its own ground before it invites others to plant seeds of hope. When the stranger walks into a church, he or she must feel that here is a place where people can face conflict without flying apart, where differences do not lead to judgment, where diversity does not breed hatred. We create such an ethos not by seeking intimacy with each other but by letting God stand in our midst as mediator of our conflict, as guide toward the truth that unites. If we lack faith that God stands among us, consensus will not work; we will constantly try to manipulate the outcome rather than let ourselves be led. If we lack faith that God stands between us we will never welcome the stranger; we will respond with defensiveness and fear rather than openness to this chance to serve and be served. The church will practice the public life not simply by proper programming, not simply by right belief. The church will practice the public life by practicing the presence of God, a presence in which gaps are bridged, wounds healed, obstacles surmounted, in which the many become one.

From a paper prepared for a workshop on lay ministry at Christ Church, Little Rock.

by the Rev. N. Patrick Murray, Rector

Some years ago I visited an Episcopal church in Ohio. this parish had decided to make a theological statement with its architecture, and it was unforgettable. The church was located on a busy street, and the entire back of the church was glass, from high cathedral roof to the floor. Why did they choose this architectural form? In order to say that the church must never shut out the world. The busy thoroughfares of the "wild world" must remain visible to us, even as we worship. The glass wall created a powerful sense of being with God in his world, not cut off from it.

I wonder sometimes what would happen if we took out the stained glass windows behind our altars, and put in *plain* glass ones. As we partake of the Lord's body and blood, would we better understand his words, "This bread which I shall give *for the life of the world* is my flesh." (Jn. 6:51)

May I offer a somewhat inelegant but rather accurate analogy to illustrate the relationship of the church and the world. The church is a service station! Now a car will run for a while without having to be serviced, but not for long. It has to have its energy (fuel) supply replenished. It has to have broken parts repaired. It has to be renewed—new tires, oil, and water. Otherwise it will soon be unable to fulfill its purpose.

But no one in his right mind buys a car in order to take it to the service station. No normal person wants to keep his car around the service station all the time. Service stations are a means to an end. They provide what we need to continue our journey, to get back into the world, and to keep moving toward our destination.

To be sure, it is very important that *some* people be willing to train themselves for work at the service station, and offer themselves in that vocation. They are absolutely essential. But just think what would happen if *everybody* got the idea that the only true vocation was to work at a service station!

So it is with the church. There are absolutely vital and indispensable ministries that go on within its walls: sacramental, educational, administrative, and social. But it is a terrible mistake to think that these make up the *real* ministry of the church. No, the church building or institution, is merely the place where we get renewed and repaired to do Christ's work *in the world*. That is where he came, and lived, and died, and after death poured out his living spirit—in the world which he created. "For God so loved the world," St. John reminded us, "that he gave his only begotten son" to save it. That is why we the church can never hide in the wild wood, like Mr. Rat and Mr. Mole, and ignore the wild world beyond!

Now there is one inescapable conclusion from all of this, and that is that the work of the church primarily must be the ministry of the laity. It is primarily the *laos* of God who must "go forth in the name of Christ" to serve as his ambassadors of reconciliation in the world. The reconciling of the world to Christ must happen in homes, offices, classrooms, playgrounds, factories, businesses, schools—wherever people are working, struggling, deciding, hurting, and hoping.

It is here that God's work is to be done, not always in churchy words or overtly religious language, but in loving deeds, quality of life, struggling for peace and justice, integrity, and genuine caring. It is here that people read "the fifth gospel," which for many is the only gospel they have ever read. The fifth gospel is us—our lives lived in the world.

Where in the World is the Church?

by Celia A. Hahn

The Church as a World in Itself is a closed system, rigid and static, with the world out of sight. A triangle, a rigid structure, is a natural symbol for a hierarchical institution. The few at the top, not surprisingly, want to preserve their power. All those further down acknowledge the position of the higher-ups and may covet it. These drives give the structure rigidity and stability. Because of this structure's enduring nature, the past seems to point the way to the future. Avery Dulles describes the institutional view of the church as "a world view in which everything remains essentially the same as it was when it began, and by which origins are therefore all-important."[1] Unchanging structures may comfort those of us who crave a high level of control, but they leave us unable to listen to the surprisingly new word of God that turns things upside down.

The rigid boundaries show clearly who is "in" and who is "out." Communication across the boundaries is difficult, partly because the attention of the institution is pretty steadily focused on ecclesiastical matters—on what is going on within the walls of the church—and these preoccupations seem trivial to those outside the walls. Civic leaders in Hartford, Connecticut, used words like " 'passive,' 'reactive,' 'irrelevant,' 'timid,' 'antiseptic,' 'selfish,' 'weak,' and 'uninvolved,' " to describe the posture of churches toward public issues.[2] The Closed Church's attention is directed toward the insiders. Outsiders are seen as important if they are candidates for membership. Those who leave are ignored or discredited.

So the Closed Church sees itself, first and foremost, as an institution, and focuses on its own ecclesiastical concerns. As Verna Dozier puts it, "Instead of the structures being tools to help the people, the people become subservient to the structures."[3] The institutional church, not the world, is "where the action is." Financial resources are heavily committed to the support of institutional purposes. People are considered "faithful" when they "support the church" and put a good deal of energy into church programs. So the church itself really becomes the client, in its relationship with its members, who are busy helping the church. In her interviews with laity, Jean Haldane encountered a number of people who really did not want to involve themselves heavily with church work, and who wondered if there could possibly be any other way to belong.[4] The norm that belonging means helping the church has traditionally been accepted unquestioningly by women. Women parishioners told Nancy Van Scoyoc that they hesitated to express their own needs, and felt guilty when the demands of their roles as wives, mothers, daughters, employees, neighbors, friends, etc. forced them to turn down requests for help with church programs.[5]

In the Closed Church, wisdom is dispensed by the professionals, who know, to the laity, who do not know. Clergy tell, and laity listen. The knowledge about the meaning of life that matters is owned and dispensed by the church. Seminary president George Peck describes his realization "that as an ordained person I had never really learned to *hear* the laity. I had become much too accustomed simply to *talking* to them."[6] It is not surprising that clergy would see religious truth as an arcane subject owned by professional theologians, since they themselves were trained in seminaries, where they went to learn from the experts, and from which they went forth to carry their new expertise to those who needed it. Wisdom flows from the top downward. It also tends to flow from the head.

The assumption that lay people do not know anything important for the church to find out about is revealed by the surprise laity evidence when they are asked, and by the surprise clergy express when they are told something useful by laity. Interviewees typically betrayed astonishment that anyone would want to know about their experiences and thoughts. They were sharing their stories for the first time; the church had not previously shown any interest in them.[7] One clergyman asked his flock some questions about how the church was coming across to them: "What do you like?" "What do you miss?" "It's *amazing*," he said, "how the people in your congregation can come up with the answers!"[8]

If church leaders are already in possession of all the knowledge that matters, they will not waste their time asking questions of those who live most of their lives outside the church. The position of lay people in the Closed Church is analogous to the position of students in schools or patients in hospitals. Conventionally, wisdom is not sought from school children or sick people. The very terms "student" and "sick" defines them as the "unknowing ones" in the institutions in question. But if you read "The President checked into Walter Reed," or "Churchill was a poor student," you have a clue that here is more than a patient or a student. When the world is out of sight, laity are devalued. As George Peck puts it, "The very word 'lay' implies a less than positive judgment, and expressions like 'he's only a layman' come too readily to our lips."[9] But if you had reason to respect the wisdom that person described as "only a layman" brought from his experience in a role outside the church, you might think of a number of questions you wanted to ask him.

The Closed Church doesn't ask, and generally the laity don't volunteer opinions. Nancy Van Scoyoc found that "Many difficult and painful issues profoundly affecting women's lives are not shared with the congregation or with clergy because women do not feel they are important enough and because they do not want to bother others unless the issue is critical."[10] Some interviewees were reluctant to talk about their own religious journeys because they were afraid their personal beliefs and practices would not measure up.[11] Further causes for diffidence on the part of laity may be found in their unfamiliarity with the language used by professionals and in their perception that their concerns are not the real agenda of the Closed Church. "So the whole structure communicates to the lay person, 'You do not know,' and the lay person replies, 'Yes, I do not know.'"[12]

In the Closed Church, power is a limited commodity, concentrated at the top of the system. Loren Mead describes the church's power system as clericalism, a "system that traps clergy and laity into institutional power relations that sustain a superior/inferior class distinction."[13] Since the serpent's seductive "You will be like God," we have hungered to make ourselves special. In a hierarchical system, power is seen as a scarce commodity, a fixed quantity for which many are competing. If I take two-thirds of the pie, there is only one-third left for you. So power *over* others leads naturally to distrust, competition, and even aggression. Responsibility weighs heavily at the top of the pyramid, while the responsibility of those at the bottom is extremely limited. The institution exerts control within its boundaries; the flip side is that the institution tends to focus its attention on that which it controls.

In the Closed Church, power is more important than function in distinguishing roles, but the realities of the power structure are often obscured. In top-dog/underdog power relationships, top dogs (and sometimes underdogs, too) are often heard to say that there is really no difference between the dogs. "Let's not talk about *differences* between blacks and whites, let's talk about what we have in *common*." "I'm not a feminist; I'm a humanist." "We are all just people." Those statements sound open and egalitarian. They can be used, however, to blow fog around the realities of who is calling the shots, so that neither the more powerful nor the less powerful see the power realities clearly. Because differences are kept out of sight, *functions* are hard to distinguish. Differences in functions between clergy and lay roles are not seen clearly, because power *over* others appears to be more important than power *for* accomplishing a task.

Laity are not viewed as ministers with a distinct role in the Closed Church, but as pale and inferior copies of the clergy. Lay ministry is not recognized as different in direction from clergy ministry, but takes as its model the liturgical and pastoral functions ordained ministers perform. The vested acolyte, standing by at the altar; the lay pastoral associate, seeing ministry as kindly support of individuals—these helpers may be performing useful and rewarding services. But if these roles are seen as the typical and primary expression of "lay ministry," the real distinction between clergy and lay roles has been obliterated. *It is because the world is out of sight* that lay ministry loses its distinctive direction, and fades into a support system for clergy ministry.

The ecclesiastical universe acknowledges only church work. As one laywoman put it, "the Church has only been interested in, and supportive of, the work I do *at* and *for* the Church."[14] A study of 29 urban congregations revealed that 70% of the members defined "ministry of the laity" as "doing things at church" only.[15] Dirk Rinehart writes of "remembering a medical doctor friend of mine in the United States who finally claimed his profession as a ministry after several years of being blinded to that possibility. Strangely, the primary affirmation he received from his local parish was for serving as a lay reader and singing in the choir!"[16] Another friend tells of a high official in the Department of Agriculture bringing cans to the parish collection of food for the church soup kitchen. No one saw this as a trivial gesture when compared to the power this man had to influence American policies that could alleviate world hunger. That is a clear example of the kind of blindness that can result when the church's world does not extend beyond its own door.

In the Closed Church, clergy are the subjects of ministry, and laity are the objects of ministry. Since the world is out of sight, the action is confined to the church. The clergy help the laity, and the laity help out at the church. The actors in this drama are not knights doing battle in the world, but patients, nursed by the clergy and allowed to help around the ward. As Hendrik Kraemer put it, "At best the laity was the flock: always it was object, never subject in its own calling and responsibility."[17] We betray this assumption that clergy are the subjects in the language of ownership frequently employed: "the pastor's board," "his congregation," "one of his laymen." In the Closed Church, clergy play the role of Parent, and laity play the role of Child, to use transactional analysis terms.

Clergy and executives in the Closed Church suffer from a crushing burden of responsibility, while laity suffer from being infantilized. The stress of those at the top of church hierarchies has been documented by Roy Oswald in a study of clergy who moved out of parish ministry into church executive roles and suffered a dangerously high incidence of stress-related illnesses and serious family problems. In interviews these executives reported being "overwhelmed by responsibility."[18] In a hierarchical system where distinctions between roles are based not so much on function as on the possession or lack of power, and on the presumption that those at the "top" are the "best" in some generalized way, those at the peak of the pyramid can be seduced into thinking that they are more than human, capable of producing enormous quantities of good works while requiring no support.

The forces that build and maintain this trap recycle relentlessly. Those at the apex of the power system often feel cut off and isolated from "where it's at," even though they are the leaders who are supposed to be calling the shots. The system does not encourage feedback for the man at the top. (I say "man" because there are almost no women heading church hierarchies.) And because these men are overworking at good and useful—even holy—tasks, they will be admired (though perhaps affectionately chided, praised with faint damns) for their all-consuming dedication. At the same time, the overworked church executive with his health and family problems sets powerful norms that can reinforce works-righteousness for everybody. The stress level is intensified because nobody will level with the top dog, but the underdogs will aim all the anger and frustration they have been nursing toward the system his way.

It isn't necessary to reach into the ranks of bishops and executive presbyters to see the ecclesiastical equivalent of "the White man's burden." Roy Oswald studied 102 new pastors who reported a similar workaholic life style, neglect of family, and apparent discomfort with their own finitude.[19] They complained about needing a "336 hour work week" and "a Hertz Rent-a-Family that leaves a good impression, yet needs no time." John Fletcher described the lure of being sought after as a religious leader as a heady experience which tempts the clergyperson to glory in omnipotence at the expense of rest, family life, health, and clarity about who the Savior in this parish really is.[20] The seduction of being an "omnipotent helper" discourages many clergy from living out the dependence on God they preach about on Sunday mornings. Ministers' Life Insurance ads dramatize the temptation and the burden: "Does your congregation expect you to perform miracles?" "The stress that the average minister bears would bring most people to their knees."

In church systems, the leaders tend to *overfunction*, while the laity tend to *underfunction*, to use the language employed by family systems experts like Edwin H. Friedman.[21] The relationship is not unlike that of a family in which one person—Mother, for instance— takes responsibility for everything and everybody, while other family members are somewhat depressed and do not have the space they need to grow into their full potential. In order to relieve the stress she suffers from the enormous load of responsibility she has shouldered, and to provide others with the opportunity to grow as responsible human beings, the overfunctioner will need to default, to leave some responsibilities available for the underfunctioners to pick up and own.

This distortion cycles through the whole church system. Verna Dozier points to the collusion: "What gives clergy the feeling that they ought to know everything? All too often lay people give them that feeling, and clergy feel guilty if they don't meet those unreal expectations."[22] The temptation to give away our own authority and responsibility, to throw ourselves at the feet of some idea, organization, or person who will show us *the way*, appears throughout human history. "Give us a king!" Then we won't have to suffer the fear and uncertainty that are inescapable accompaniments to being free persons in an ambiguous world. Alban Institute studies of churches between pastors revealed the "vacancy" period as an open moment in a congregation's life when laity discover, "This is our church!" When a new pastor is installed, many laity seem eager to bury that discovery as quickly as they can, sit back in relief and let the minister take over. If we laity project our own religious authority on the clergy, we have given it away, and we tell ourselves we have none, while the clergy become isolated, workaholics, lightening rods for congregational hostility. Avery Dulles points to the danger that "the priest will be viewed as a substitute for the community—as one who stays close to God so that the laity, relying on his intercession, may be worldly."[23] But being called to ordained ministry is in reality no more a unique call to a religious life than being called to be a physician is a unique call to a healthy life.

The burdens borne by clergy and laity in the Closed Church are inextricably intertwined. Clergy are made to feel like failures unless they keep laity busy with endless church programs, while laity are made to feel like failures unless they pour their energies into supporting those programs. Jean Haldane's interviewees made it clear to her that "the church does not by its behavior validate ministry outside its walls."[24] In overvaluing the religious authority of clergy,

we laity undervalue our own. In exchange for the fantasy that some-
body else is going to take care of our religious life, we receive a
mess of pottage; we end up spiritually infantilized, bereft of dignity,
relegated to a "vague and supplemental"[25] role, anxious that we may
be the only doubters in the pew. While the Gospel proclamation
affirms us as loved children of God, the Closed Church system in its
actual functioning leaves us feeling that we are really not of much
account.

There are undoubtedly many reasons why the ranks of the laity
are so heavily female. Certainly one important reason why women
have been more invested in church activities has been the time
housewives have had available for voluntary pursuits. I think there
is also a psychological congruence between the role of laity in the
Closed Church and the role of women in our society. Women have
been socialized to bow to outside pressures to "remain girls,
dependent on wiser ones to point the way," says Ann Belford Ulanov.[26] Ulanov cites Valerie Goldstein's illuminating insight that the
cardinal sin of woman is not pride, but *hiding*, "a refusal to claim
the self God has given... by hiding behind self-doubt and feelings
of inadequacy. The force of her argument arises from countless
women's experience of avoiding the self that they are, by always
assuming that some greater authority knows better, be that father,
mother, husband, even, in this case, theologians' interpretation of
sin."[27] Heeding male religious leaders' warnings against sinful
human nature's tendency to build proud towers, woman may fall
unknowing into the opposite temptation, viewing herself as a tene-
ment rather than the temple of the Holy Spirit she was created to
be. The church's infantilization of laity compounds the seduction in
this time-honored temptation of woman, impoverishing not only *her*
life, but the life of the church and of all the arenas in which she is
called to love with all her strength. She cannot rise to this calling
without first loving herself as her neighbor.

The tentative church connections of many lay men may result in
part from their ambivalence about being identified with such an
infantilized and feminized laity. To those for whom it is important
to be on top of things, to live lustily and fully, a "soft" organization
full of women may not look very appealing. Church leaders are
often heard worrying about the dwindling number of men in
churches. Many men who do participate seem careful to choose
roles like treasurer, chairman of building committees, that partake
of the character of "real men's work" in secular settings. A church
that took men's worldly work seriously as ministry, respected them
as competent adults, and did not appear to be treating them like
"wimps," might engage their more wholehearted participation.

The Church as a World in Itself: one picture, one way the church tends to function. All its parts work together. It is busy with matters within its own walls, where the clergy help the laity, and those who are only laymen (or, more likely, "girls") help the church to the best of their limited ability and knowledge. Men may be alienated, women confirmed in their disempowerment. If anyone asks the laity what they think and experience, they are surprised. Roles are confused, power realities are obscured. Everybody is hurting: those in control are burdened by the responsibility for religious life which has been abdicated by the laity (not without clergy encouragement). Laity then see themselves as they are seen—ignorant, diffident, and passive.

NOTES

1. Avery Dulles, *Models of the Church* (Doubleday, 1978), p. 36.

2. William J. McKinney, David A. Roozen, and Jackson W. Carroll, *Religion's Public Presence* (The Alban Institute, 1982), p. 11.

3. Verna J. Dozier, *Authority of the Laity* (The Alban Institute, 1982), p. 6.

4. Jean M. Haldane, *Religious Pilgrimage* (The Alban Institute, 1975), p. 13.

5. Nancy J. Van Scoyoc, *Women, Change and the Church* (Abingdon, 1980), p. 63.

6. George Peck, "Reconceiving the Ministry of the Laity," *Action Information*, Vol. VIII, No. 4, Reprinted from Laity Project Newsletter.

7. Van Scoyoc, Op. cit.

8. CBS Videotapes: Faith Without a Sanctuary (Produced as part of the 3-part series "For Our Times," aired Nov. 1, 8, 15, 1981).

9. Peck, Op. cit.

10. Van Scoyoc, Op. cit., p. 85.

11. Haldane, Op. cit., p. 85.

12. Dozier, Op. cit., p. 9.

13. Ibid., p. 1.

14. Candace Sutcliffe, "Speaking from Experience," *Centering*, Vol. I, No. 3).

15. OSCM Yearbook, quoted in *Action Information*, Vol. VII, No. 1.

16. Dirk Rinehart, unpublished manuscript.

17. Hendrik Kraemer, p. 72.

18. Roy Oswald, "Your Next Job May Kill You," *Action Information*, Vol. V, No. 5.

19. Roy Oswald, *Crossing the Boundary* (The Alban Institute, 1980).

20. John C. Fletcher, *Religious Authority in the Clergy* (The Alban Institute, 1975), p. 1.

21. Edwin H. Friedman, *Generation to Generation: Family Process in Church and Synagogue* (New York: Guilford Press, 1985)

22. Dozier, Op. cit., p. 9.

23. Dulles, Op. cit., p. 158.

24. Haldane, Op. cit., p. 19.

25. Ibid.
26. Ann Belford Ulanov, *Receiving Woman* (Westminster Press, 1981), p. 135.
27. Ibid., p. 134.

Ministries Outside the Parish

by Mark Gibbs

It is not so long ago that people talked of full-time Christian service almost exclusively in terms of the ordained, and those laity who were missionaries, evangelists or in other church employment. Today very many Anglicans accept wholeheartedly that God has also called many others who find that most of the development of their discipleship takes place within the ordinary structures of modern society: in the networks of their families and friends; in suburban, city or country neighborhoods; in their jobs, whether in the 'caring professions' or not; in their unemployment or retirement; and in their politics and social clubs, trade unions, and sports and leisure groups.

Even when these activities are local, they are often not organized by a parish.

Secular Christians

Of course "secular" and "Christian" are not totally exclusive. Even the busiest parish worker will sometimes engage in other political or cultural activities; likewise, it is very important that Christians who find that their main responsibilities under God lie in secular structures, also do their share (maybe a small, humble share) of churchly work. I have never forgotten the fine example set by an exceptionally busy space scientist. He refused to do any kind of church work, but he and his wife regularly taught an adolescent Sunday school class. That witness was important to several generations of teenagers.

Nevertheless, it would have been very wrong if that man had proved to be a dedicated church school teacher and an unthought-ful, irresponsible, unpolitical scientist. It would also have been wrong for his local congregation to honor him for his church work, and to ignore his spiritual needs in his exacting occupation. Yet this might easily have happened. Again and again churches tend to emphasize the churchly and to forget, or in subtle ways downgrade, Christian work and witness which is not parish-based. I want to suggest that true Christian worship and effective Christian love will always emphasize our ministry in our occupations come Monday morning.

There is, however, a strong bias towards the churchly, deeply rooted in our present liturgies and customs of worship, and reflected in many of our Anglican church organizations. Such a bias is often strengthened, maybe unconsciously, by clergy who are themselves very much parish-based. This can lead to a deep dissatisfaction felt by many lay people about the ways in which they are still regarded as less dedicated, less "holy," because they are less involved in parish activities. In actual fact, they are called to be God's witnesses in many difficult, ambiguous, and spiritually dangerous human situations. If the church is to keep their loyalty—even a critical loyalty—then we must speak to their conditions, and be careful not to choke them by laying more church work on them.

First, we must strongly affirm them and their particular discipleships. It is distressing how often even the new liturgies of many churches, including our own Anglican ones, are relatively weak in this matter. We need a strong service of affirmation, perhaps for use at the age when young people become independent, and then annually after that. And we need more about Monday morning in our ordinary Sunday worship than we ordinarily have.

Some congregations have learned most effectively how to elevate, through praise and prayer, the dispersion of the people during the week in all their different occupations and activities. Some seem ignorant of the jobs, political work and leisure interests represented in their midst. Some parishes only list people according to their church involvements; how many display a local and city map showing not only where people live but also where they work?

Second, we must listen to these less churchly laity. Some of them have considerable doubts about some traditional parts of the faith, and are decidedly skeptical about the effectiveness of the organized churches. Others are more conservative. Their ideas about God may be a worried muddle about meek Jesus and stern Jehovah. Their styles of prayer may seem distinctly childish, their ideas about the Bible dated and sketchy, but whether they are radical or conservative, theologically or politically, they are God's front line troops. They go daily where priests, teachers and writers venture only occasionally, and by courtesy; so the worship and learning activities and the whole thinking of their parishes must emphasize their develop-

ment into a committed adult laity. Professor Harvey Cox, Professor
of Divinity at Harvard Divinity School, comments from one of his
books: "The Christian army is the one where the only people to be
trained properly are the chaplains and the musicians."

The concerns of these apparently more secular lay people must
come out in the open. They, like everybody else, must learn how to
deal with God's demands for their particular jobs and lives. Adult
Christian commitment means an *informed* commitment; it is not a
matter of being loyal sheep. It has been wonderful to find, in recent
years, so many lay people—scientists, factory workers, teachers,
doctors, politicians, policemen, military people—learning to argue
very profitably about their Christian responsibilities and learning to
act on their new convictions. The church must help them do this,
both in parish and in wider groups. It must never stifle such discussions just because they can be uncomfortable ones. And it must
always be remembered how important such laity are in evangelism
(properly understood). They are in contact with so many people
right outside of faith. And they can often detect, before the church
can, the compromises which the institution may make with the values of society.

The Unattached Christians

All this, however, assumes that such laity are still actively connected
with one parish or another. This assumption is false. For one reason
or another, the churches in Britain, and even our own Church of
England, seem extremely reluctant to come to terms with the
unpleasant fact that a great many people who call themselves Christians only worship occasionally. Their links with any denomination
are, at best, tenuous. I am not referring to the large number of English people who must be considered nominal believers, or who
would describe themselves as agnostics. (It is not for us to judge
them.) What I want to suggest is that we reckon more seriously than
we do with the considerable army of our fellow citizens who sin-
cerely (though often very modestly) call themselves Christians; who
try to follow God as revealed in Jesus Christ, but who have simply
dropped out of institutional church membership. Of course, if they
are responding in any way to the call of Almighty God, they are, in
some sense, to be numbered with the saints as part of the great
church of Jesus Christ (though they might well find such language
uncomfortable). But they don't want to be members of the parish of
St. Marmaduke's, or of Toddlewick Methodist, or of the local
Friends Meeting House. I must admit that most of my family and

many of my friends and their children have been Christians of this unattached kind. I find that they often wanted to say "Yes" to Jesus Christ, but "No, thank you" to the churches.

Such unattached Christians are now commonly found all over Europe, all over North America, and in many urban areas of the Third World. In some countries, they may represent 50 per cent of the Christians. They pose a major threat to most of our traditional beliefs about the need for institutional church membership, and to many plans for highly organized, well-financed Anglican structures. It is not surprising that sometimes church leaders rather hotly denounce them as "disloyal." It is, however, much more profitable to learn to respect them, to listen to them, and to talk with them.

Yes, we must respect them, for often we will find that their Christian ministries are outstanding, both in their personal caring and neighborliness and in their truly sacrificial involvement in politics and social action. We must honor their often costly and lonely attempts at personal discipleship, perhaps together with, perhaps without, their spouses and children. What they know about the Gospel is often translated quickly and sharply into personal and political commitment. Many of them may well be on the fringes of the churches but at the heart of the Kingdom. It is simply impertinent to dismiss them out of hand as inferior or uninformed believers; and disgraceful when church goers denounce them when they do attend a Christmas or Easter church service.

We must also find ways of listening to such people. Indeed we will have to be particularly careful to help them speak out honestly, for English people are inclined to put kindliness and tactfulness before truthfulness, especially in matters of religion. These non-parish Christians are often very anxious not to offend. They don't easily tell us why they find church membership unsatisfying, they just slip quietly away (75 per cent of them before the age of 20, according to the new BCC (British Council of Churches) Youth Study of 1984).

Of course we want to testify that regular worship can mean as much to them as it does to us; of course we want to emphasize that the Christian faith is a matter of living together and not just a private matter; of course we long for them to find deep satisfaction in active membership of a lively parish. But let us first listen! Then, indeed, we will learn that things do not look like that at all to many of them. If we say, "There are such riches to be found in regular Anglican worship and you are missing all the strengths of Christian fellowship," they may quite calmly reply, "Yes, of course, that's true for those who like that kind of thing. Nothing at all against it! But for many reasons, it's not for us."

Sometimes it is a matter of cultural or class style. There are questions of language—not necessarily old versus new—and deep problems about church music. Often it is a matter of age groups: how can lively teenagers join a congregation that has an average age of 50 or 60? There are some gender questions here too: very many English *men* prefer to have a church to stay away from. Often unattached Christians see our local congregation as a genteel club not suitable for rougher, less formal people (and certainly not for ordinary workers).

Even when we protest—as I think we should—that occasional church attendees often expect a very traditional style liturgy from 1662, complete with "Rock of Ages," and have no idea of what Christian worship can mean to modern people, we must accept that many parishes are not very good at communicating such insights to outsiders. This is indeed very serious.

Questions to be Faced

Frankly, many of these Christians no longer feel guilty about not being regular church members. They don't feel that they are missing much. I hope we can convince them otherwise, but this can only come about through a candid exploration of some very tricky questions with them. For example:

1. What is really compulsory about Christian worship, and what is optional? We believe that God calls us to regular, public worship, not only to a private and personal belief (even if this is worked out in solidarity with others working for a just society). We believe that an essential element of Christian living is a sharing of insights, of successes and failures with other believers. Individual Christians can be lonely and despondent, cranky, theologically feeble. The fellowship of believers is meant to give us both support and mutual criticism. But it is quite another matter to justify from these arguments many of our present denominational and cultural church traditions.

2. What should we accept in the way of informal house groups and house churches? A good many Christians now affirm that they find in these exactly those qualities of support and mutual caring which they maintain they don't find in ordinary parishes.

3. What can we learn from those retreat centers and programs abroad like the Kirchentags, the enormous German lay congresses and "lay academies" which do attract many unattached believers, and apparently help them to gain spiritual strength and wisdom?

4. What is the place of the family as a center of Christian fellow-

ship, worship and learning? Some non-parish Christians find great strength today in worshipping together with families and friends.

We can easily understand the concern and indeed the resentment felt by many faithful church people about this kind of question. How can our great church structures be financed, how can our priests be trained, how can scriptural truths and church traditions be learned, without a network of formal local parishes? We have a right to expect that our unattached fellow Christians listen to such arguments. They must try to realize that it matters much to many Anglicans that they have opted out.

But this must be a true dialogue, not another attempt to burden them with guilt for letting down God and the church. And since it is now some 200 years since these arguments began openly, in England and in many Western countries, it is urgent that our Church of England give these matters further attention. Otherwise we shall lose many opportunities of making allies of some of the most sincere Christians in the land.

"No Moment During the Week is 'Recess' from Ministry"

by Barbara Campbell

"Lay Ministry." What images do you see? Do you picture the layreader competently reading the lessons? Do you picture the Altar Guild member serving faithfully? Do you picture the person who always helps at the church?

Or perhaps, have we journeyed to the point where we can see lay ministers when we look at ourselves in the mirrors of our lives? My mirrors are in my home where I also see my family reflected. My mirrors are the windows that don't open in the high school which reflect my students surrounding me. Perhaps your mirrors reflect you and the friends with whom you relax.

We, the lay people, are ministers and minister. How do we get to that point of realization? Consider the beginning four small babies had a Sunday not too long ago.

Bundled against the mid-winter wind, the infants and their families filled the front pews at the 11:00 service. An occasional cry interrupted the Gospel which recalled the baptism of Jesus, the descent of the Holy Spirit and the identifying voice, "On you my favor rests." (Lk 3:22) The sermon caught the double focus of baptism, the welcoming of new Christians and the renewal and deepening of our own commitment to Christ.

The babies, in quilted white satin suit and long white dresses trimmed with lace, were carried to the font. Bonnets were removed. Families and the congregation gathered around.

As we listened and watched the tiny ones, we prayed that the newly baptized (and we) would be filled with the holy and life giving Spirit; that they (and we) would be kept in the faith and communion of the Church; that they (and we) would be taught to love others in the power of the Spirit; and that they (and we) would be sent into the world to witness to that love.

The children were handed from parent to priest. "Amanda Rachael, I baptize you in the name of the Father. ..." "Kyle Thomas, you are sealed by the Holy Spirit in Baptism. . . ." "Joshua Matthew, you are marked as Christ's own forever." The candle was given to the parents of Meagan Elisabeth. "Receive the light of Christ. May it burn brightly in her life."

We exchanged the Peace and opened ourselves again to the gifts of baptism as we prayed, "Give them (and us) an inquiring and discerning heart" (the attitude that asks why and seeks meaning), "the courage to will and to persevere" (strength to question the status quo and to lead), "a spirit to know and to love you" (the grounding of all ministerial action), "and the gift of joy and wonder in all your works" (joy that creation is our place of ministry and all of creation is God's).

That's strong empowerment and so it is intended to be. It is empowerment that legitimizes and gives license to lay ministry.

As we watched the new Christians being carried down the aisle by the rector, they began their ministry by ministering. How did they do that? They're only infants! They ministered by being themselves. There's no pretense to a newly baptized child.

What did they do? They created community. We relaxed. We exchanged smiles. With greater warmth, cohesiveness, we turned to the altar to move to the Service of the Table.

"The Lord be with you."

"And also with you."

The familiar versicle and response is an interaction which expresses mutuality, both key factors in understanding ministry. Ministry seen as service is only half the definition. It is a combination of being as well as doing; of who a person is as well as what that person does.

We who are Christians receive our identification at baptism and reaffirm it as we witness baptisms and each time we receive Communion. Being and doing intentionally combine in interaction with other people. Ministry is that interaction which opens people to the experience of God's love with all its attributes of justice and peace.

Where We Minister

Does a lay person minister within the walls of the church to church members or does the lay person minister as we interact Monday through Friday wherever we may be? Because we are Anglicans, the answer is both/and. The laity do minister within the church walls in necessary ways which preserve and promote the institution.

These are the readily recognized lay ministries—singing in the choir, administering the chalice, calling on the sick, preparing the budget, and going to Vestry meetings. Without these lay efforts, the institutional church would lose its present form and have to change its functioning.

The exercise of these efforts is ministry and, even within the walls of the church, needs to be called ministry rather than just a meeting attended, turkey roasted, or church school class taught. Naming what we do for what it is is a good step towards acceptance of ourselves as ministers.

The Eucharist at the parish altar centers us, nourishes us, and directs us into the world. At the end of every Eucharist and especially the ones following baptisms, do we hear the words of the dismissals, "Go forth into the world," "Go. . .to love and serve the Lord" as the words of a player/coach sending the team out onto the field? Do we see ourselves as the players?

In the World

Consider the world where I, a lay person, am. On a daily basis, I interact with 1,500 kids in the high school. I sign the attendance card when the 16-year-old mother of two returns after an absence. I directed the play before 600 people at the Madrigal Feaste. I helped the Junior Class sell Mickey Mouse hats and balloons for Spirit Week. I volunteered for the committee charged with establishing trust and improving communication with and involvement of the high school staff in decision-making. I guided my students through I-Search Research Papers and saw them open up, challenge themselves and enjoy the work.

You may negotiate the multimillion dollar contract, run the car pool, or work in the plant that is or was on strike. You and I are the church scattered into all parts of God's creation interacting daily with all of God's people. We, who are in the world, are in just the right places to be and to function as ministers every day.

How We Minister

How, then, do we act when we minister in the world? Do I start prayer groups before school? Do I put up religious posters in my classroom? I don't. What is important is that we Christians who are in the world are already "doing" what we are intended to do in order to minister. We are interacting now. To exercise lay ministry, we do not have to "do more." We need to become more conscious of what we are doing and make our actions more intentional and without pretense. We need to know and understand our motivation.

Community Context and Support of Lay Ministry

Just as it is from the parish altar that we are sent into the world, so
to it is within the parish that support for lay ministry can be the
strongest. We need a community within the worshipping parish
where we can tell our story to people who are open to listening,
sharing and growing in the faith.

Personally, I need a community which values the interactions I
have with students, other teachers, administrators and parents. I
need to see my life in perspective and connected to the tradition of
the church. I need to be both challenged and affirmed in my
actions and reflection. I need to be involved with others in the process of theological reflection on our ministries. I need to regularly
worship—whether that be from the pew, the lectern, the officiant's
desk, or the communion rail.

These needs are being met now in my parish, through its worship services, its people, its clergy, my mentoring an Education for
Ministry (EFM) seminar for eight years, and personal reading. As I
need to be open and to grow, I seek new opportunities and deeper
understandings.

Does acceptance of the gifts of baptism mean I can now go off
on my own and preach, heal, and teach? Not really! There is a big
difference between "going off on my own" and "being sent by
myself." We are empowered because we are a part of a community
whose life centers around the altar in the middle of the parish. It is
the community of that parish which sends us into our several
worlds.

Progressing in Lay Ministry

The change is basically growth from the disbelief of "Who? Me,
Lord?" to the agonizing of "Why me, Lord?" to the resurrected spirit
of "Here I am, send me." That change, for me—the rare breed who
is a born Episcopalian—is still evolving in a vacillating manner. I
feel I have finally passed the "Who? Me, Lord?" stage.

Growing steps in that stage were the experience of candlelight
Christmas Eve services at the Cathedral in Hartford, national Canter-
bury conferences with 500 other college students, and the influence
of people who believed, listened and shared. (Other moments such
as flunking my test for confirmation and five years of avoiding the
Institutional Church just validate my vacillation!)

It's easier in the "Why me, Lord?" stage. I carry with me the
Hagar cartoon, now yellowed after being on my office wall for two

years. In it, Hagar's Viking ship is sinking, it's raining, lightening is striking and Hagar cries out, "Why me?" The response from the storm clouds, which I love, is, "Why not?"

I accept that challenge every once in a while and say "Send me" as I chose to return to the high school after a confrontation (and as I chose to write this article!) As I choose to become more involved, I see vindication, new roles opening, new outpouring of love and situations for rejoicing. It isn't easy. Everything isn't all right. It is exciting. It is comforting. The sense of going "cum fortis," with strength, is real.

Let's you and me . . . Let us (the lay people of the church), accept being sent by the parish community to go in peace to love, to serve, to minister to the Lord wherever in God's creation we find ourselves.

The Theological Issues

All four articles in this section were originally published in the
Alban Institute's Action Information.
    *Patricia Garrett Drake asks "Are Laity Being Shortchanged?" and
focuses on two areas where the church is seriously deficient in its
response to its lay members—in its education of the ordained and
in the theological education of its laity.*
    *The next article is a concrete example of both failures: "A Sacred
Space."*
    The third begins to lay the ground for a "Theology of the Laity."
    *And the fourth article is a design to help people begin a Biblical-
ly based struggle with the issue.*

Are laity being shortchanged?

by Patricia Garrett Drake

I want to share with you what I understand to be some of the needs of lay people and their expectations and hopes for the future of seminaries. I would like to focus on two issues that I have heard the most about in my encounters with lay people.

First: The concept of ministry as taught by the seminary is lopsided. Second: Laity desperately need and want theological insight for living their lives and they are not getting it.

Let me go further. The concept of ministry as taught by the seminary reinforces the image of the congregation as an end in itself. It reinforces a pastor-centered ministry to sick and troubled laity. The congregation is not an end in itself! The pastor is not the center of ministry! The laity are not sick and troubled although there are times when we will need help, just as clergy will.

Lay people have an urgent need for ongoing, open and honest joint inquiry into the relationships between our lives in the world and traditional theology. The knowledge of our Judeo-Christian heritage which has been ladled out to us in bits and pieces over the years is not sufficient to deal with the complexity of our lives.

I have recently been involved in two research projects which have colored my understanding of both the seminary and the congregation. These experiences have confirmed my skepticism in both arenas. My skepticism has to do with the fact that over and over in my life in the congregation and in contact with seminaries I have gotten the feeling that whatever is going on "does not apply"—that in some way it is out of context. Working on these projects and listening to other lay people have helped me to understand that my "seat of the pants" instincts have not been wrong. They have also given me a vision that has heightened my sense of hope about both institutions.

The project with which I have been involved for the past three years took a look at how groups of laity, generally called lay train-

ing committees or intern committees, are being used in field education programs in seminaries. (See reports of this project listed in
the catalogue on p. 15.) I feel as though I have been working both
sides of the street and that has been important.

I vividly recall my own first encounter with the seminary as a
member of one of these groups. I had gone on campus to be
trained to help guide a student through her internship in my parish.
The three-hour session was planned in a manner which allowed little feedback to the seminary. I particularly remember being told
that I should have a "meaningful dialogue" with this student and I
kept frantically searching through the afternoon for a handle on
what this "meaningful dialogue" was to be about! It never came,
though I did receive some broad hints on what the seminary was
interested in. The focus was to be on the student's style of ministry
in the parish. The context of that ministry was to be the congregation. Wait a minute! My context is not the congregation! My context
as a lay person is the world! Where do the clergy learn about that?

Sometimes, and I believe, most often, they never do learn. The
process by which students are educated and become ordained continually reinforces the perception of the congregation as the end
rather than the means. It is no wonder then that we do not feel
successful in "bridging the gap between theory and practice." We
have identified the congregation rather than the world as the arena
for "practice" and the clergy rather than the "whole people of God"
as the principal practitioner. If one footing of the span, the bridge,
is our Judeo-Christian heritage (theory) we have ignored the other
footing—the world—in our attempt to bridge theory and practice,
and stopped at an intermediate support—the congregation. We
have effectively created a cantilevered structure—a span connected
and supported at only one end—a kind of spiritual diving board,
because the connection at the other end is seldom correctly identified, much less analyzed. Few students, and therefore few clergy,
have experience of the world to which they need to connect.

How little students understand of the complexity of the world
was brought home to me recently. One of our seminary students in
my own parish was talking to one of the parishioners when he
hailed me and said, "How can I convince Albert here of his lay ministry?" He continued, "Albert works with figures." On inquiring further I found that Albert, still speechless, worked at the World Bank.

The lay committee project reinforced for me how we continually
miss the point of what we are about. At the end of the project, we
went back to one seminary to tell the faculty and staff what we had
found. I stated one finding that had held true without fail: In the lay
training committees, the more lay people were learning about their

own lives and tradition, the more the student was learning about his or her role as an ordained minister. The research team had also reached some conclusions about ways to enhance the possibility of learning occurring in the group. The main point was that the focus of the group not be entirely on the student's ministry within the parish but also on the ministry of the whole people of God in terms of the committee members' lives and their own ministry in the world. A faculty leader of the seminary we were visiting became very angry and spent a good deal of time explaining to me that the task of the seminary was not to educate lay people. He also emphasized the dangers of encouraging lay people to ask "what's in this for me?" Where then is the interconnectedness between students and laity we found so central in our study? The connection often gets lost in the shuffle. Before an interview with one student, a group of about six of us were seated at the end of two six-foot tables pushed together end to end. The student came in, introduced himself and sat down at the far end of one of the tables twelve feet away from the six of us clustered at the other end. He proceeded to tell us with great excitement that his internship has been invaluable to him because it had taught him so much about working with small groups!

After auditing a course on "lay ministry" at the seminary, one woman commented to me that one great learning has emerged for her. She said, "The church is a talking institution, ready to go out and proclaim. But because we seldom listen we most often proclaim in a vacuum. Clergy learn the skills of talking but one must learn to listen before anything can be said that is relevant."

The second project which has given me further insight into this lack of vision and inability to listen was called "Women in Transition." This research project was an attempt to look at the lives of women in local congregations who have undergone various types of transition in their lives in the past four years. The focus of the study was to identify the ways the congregation supported the women during these changing times. The results of the study showed that the church most often encourages only certain types of life experiences to be dealt with within the church structure. Death and illness are experiences for which the church has a format. Other transition experiences encountered in the world were seldom allowed to surface. The study showed that women simply "quietly coped" with these decision points in their lives—dilemmas about their jobs, pressures they were feeling from the church because of their decreased time and participation, time management and support systems, to name a few.

The church's perception of the scope of issues that are of concern to lay people must be broadened to include those other than physical death and illness. One person told me, "Don't give any medical analogies. Clergy already believe it is their job to help me because I am sick. I am not sick! I am alive and well and living in Washington! But my life is an active and purposeful one and I do find myself on the horns of a dilemma more often than not. And they are thorny issues. The clergy are arrogant about what the world is about. This is not their area of expertise. But they must learn to respect the complexity of the world and they must learn about it from those people who are working in it—not just the lame, the halt and blind."

One need of lay people flows into the other. Clergy and lay people alike are faced with incredibly complicated problems to which the organized church continually gives simplistic answers. I spend an evening once a week in a theological education by extension class in which we are beginning to look at a method for "identifying the issue" in an encounter brought in by someone in the group. After much effort we decide upon the issue on which we want to focus and begin to bring some of our own experiences to it. To that we add our meager but growing knowledge of the tradition. It is a very amateurish effort to connect our lives and our heritage. But it is the best guidance we have ever had for looking at our lives in light of our tradition in an ongoing systematic way, and we will get better at it. We are often called on by the seminary to "think theologically" about our lives. I do not believe we can do that without some idea of how to identify the issues and without some systematic study of our heritage. The seminary gives little evidence that it or its students can give us any help at this point. Indeed, I see little evidence that the seminary thinks theologically about its own life or task.

It is the hope, need and expectation of the laity that the concept of ministry as being taught and modeled by the seminary will change. We laity desperately need and want theological insights into how we live our lives.

A Sacred Space

by Verna J. Dozier

I was at a conference recently that concluded with a eucharist. We had been working all day in one room, and the eucharist began in that room with the liturgy of the Word. At the end of it, we were told that we would all participate in making the "sacred space." (Where we were was not a "sacred space.") So we joined hands and danced our way from that room, through another room to pick up the communion vessels, the bread and the wine, to a third room where the table was prepared, and we celebrated the eucharist in a "sacred space."

There was good reason to move to another room. There was a piano there, and singing was to be a joyful part of the eucharist.

The way we moved was creative and delightful. The room chosen was also a room in which we had lived some life together. We had eaten our meals there.

The troubling part to me was the suggestion, however subtle, that the "sacred place" was a place different from where life was lived, that the "sacred place" is where the institutionally ordained preside.

I believe the "sacred space" is where the institutionally ordained preside. I believe it is also where mothers tend their children, teachers guide their students, doctors care for their patients, police officers patrol the streets, executives make decisions, laborers ply their trades—laity everywhere doing the work they are called to do.

The ground on which we stand is holy ground.

God is where we are. What space could be more sacred than where God is? As long as we, intentionally or unintentionally, believe and therefore act out that we have to go somewhere special to meet God or do something special to be close to God, lay people will see themselves as second class citizens in the household of faith and the work they do as second class activity, their work not a calling, themselves not called.

The sacred space the clergy provide is to give lay people the opportunity to celebrate together the God we have met in the sacred places of their homes and offices and communities, to confess our failures to identify what God has made sacred, to be renewed so that we know all our life is holy.

No other understanding of the "sacred space," it seems to me, takes seriously the ministry of the laity.

Toward a Theology of the Laity

by Verna J. Dozier

There are two churches: the Church, the institution, and the Church, the People of God.

In the Church, the institution, there are two orders, clergy and lay. In the Church, the People of God, there are varieties of gifts and functions.

The two are NOT identical. The institution is the earthen vessel in which the treasure is kept. It is NOT the treasure.

Years ago in his excellent but largely ignored *A Theology of the Laity*, Hendrik Kraemer said raising the issue of lay ministry necessitated a new ecclesiology. Jesus was also aware that new wine needed new wineskins. The old vessels just could not do.

The old vessel of the institutional Church will not do if the Church is to be the Church, the People of God.

The last statement is not to say we don't need the institutional Church. It is to say we need a right perspective on the institutional Church. The institutional Church is very necessary, has always been necessary, in time will always be necessary. Without it the Church, the People of God, would not exist. The institutional Church is God's instrument for preserving God's people. Without institutionalization the Bible would never have been written, but early in the New Testament we see the beginning of the same damaging signs of institutionalization in the New Israel that the Old Testament traces in the Old Israel.

The institutional Church is subject to all the sin of any other institution: pride and arrogance and ordering and counting its life more important than anything else.

Someone has said you can tell the purpose of an organization by looking at what it measures. What does the institutional Church measure? The number of people on the rolls. The number of baptisms. The size of the collection. The number of services. The number ordained.

And it thinks these figures are an expression of its concern for spreading the Gospel. It sees spreading the Gospel in such manageable terms as saying certain words to certain folks. Those words rarely call into question the Church's investment in slum properties, silence in the face of nuclear destruction, exploitation of the helpless. The institutional Church today as in the time of Jesus rushes to the precipice Him who would proclaim deliverance to captives and liberty to the bruised.

The institutional Church can get into that liberation business only very cautiously because it has to maintain itself; and people who have the power to say yea or nay are not going to sit still for that kind of rocking the boat. Rome still bestrides the world like a mighty colossus, and the institutional Church still says, "It is better for one man to die than that a whole nation should perish."

These are not absolutely unredeemed stances, however pejoratively I have expressed them. They are just the best the institution can do. When it pretends to be more than that, when it will not face its limitations, then it is destructive.

I have a friend, who is a good priest, who always talks about balancing the needs of the institution and the needs of the individual. In that creative tension the institution is probably at its best.

But there is more than that creative tension. That is the best the Church as an institution can do. The Church as the People of God can do more. It can change the world.

But that Church is a sleeping giant, and that Church must be unbound.

The New Testament Church produced the New Testament, and threaded throughout those "loving memories" we catch glimpses of the institutionalization of that Church. It is difficult to make definitive statements about that organization, so much so that every modern form of Church organization can see in the meager record justification for its own polity, as J. R. Nelson, former Secretary of the World Council of Churches, says. Some see the threefold order of bishop, priest and deacon; others recognize only an essential presbyterate; still others discern the autonomous local congregation in which there were different kinds of ministry only for convenience.

In Matthew 16:18, Jesus says to Peter, after his confession of faith, "Thou art Peter and upon this rock I will build my church; and the gates of hell shall not prevail against it," and then he goes on to say in verse 18, "And I will give unto thee the keys of the kingdom of heaven: and whatever thou shalt bind on earth shall be bound in heaven: and whatsoever thou shalt loose on earth shall be loosed in heaven." In Matthew 18:17, the very same words are used: "Verily I say unto you, Whatsoever ye shall bind on earth shall be bound in heaven: and whatsoever ye shall loose on earth shall be loosed in heaven." But this time the words are addressed to Christians assembled together—the Church, the People of God.

Buttrick, the *Interpreter's Bible* expositor for Matthew, frankly admits the verses give the expositor trouble. Leaving the question of Peter's leadership aside, the very different placing of the same words indicate a shift in organizational structure.

Kraemer says, "The Church cannot but be also an institution. But this is the perennial thorn in the flesh, because the Church is essentially a 'colony of heaven,' a divine new beginning on the earth and in the reality of the world, a 'trek' and not an established institution." However difficult it will be for clergy and laity alike, it seems to me essential to understand the differences between the Church as an institution and the Church as the People of God, if the ministry of the laity is ever to be let loose in the world with New Testament power.

It was a people, not an institution, to whom the promise was given that they should be witnesses in Jerusalem and in all Judea, and in Samaria, and unto the uttermost parts of the earth. It was to a people, not an institution, that Peter waxes lyrical: "Ye are a chosen generation, a royal priesthood, an holy nation, a peculiar people; that ye should show forth the praises of him who called you out of darkness into his marvelous light."

If the Church is the People and not the institution, it seems to me some significant implications follow at once:

1. What happens on Sunday morning is not half so important as what happens on Monday morning. In fact what happens on Sunday morning is judged by what happens on Monday morning. If the people who gather for word and sacrament go back to that world unchanged and unchanging, they have participated in empty ritual. The worship of the Church is to nourish and strengthen ("comfort" means "with strength"), stir up and cheer the ones wearied in the struggle.

2. It is the lay people who are the key agents in the ministry of reconciliation. The clergy are the support system. It is the priesthood of the laity—lay people offering themselves in sacrificial service for the world for which Christ was willing to die—that will speak to that world of what God has done for it. It is the call of the clergy to "equip the saints," enable lay people to know who they are, tend the holy fire before which their souls may be rekindled when the flame burns low.

3. There are no second-class citizens in the household of God. Religious authority comes with baptism, and it is nurtured by prayer, worship, Bible study, life together. Indicative of the tragic confu-

sion of the two churches, for me, is that as clergy assumed institutional power (did the things necessary to keep the shop running),
lay people gave up to them religious authority as well. And of
course the clergy took it, because they could run things with much
less trouble if there weren't a lot of people sure of their stake in
the operation to cry, "Hold!" If you can convince me that only you
have the direct line to God and that I can speak to God only
through you or as you direct and that you know better what is good
for me than I do myself, and if I buy that heresy (for heresy it is!), I
give up my spiritual birthright. Religious authority is of God.
Human beings do not give it. Human beings cannot take it away.
Sinful human beings, however, can surrender it.

4. The clergy are also part of the Church, the People of God;
and therefore their first, their prime loyalty should be to the
Church, the People of God. Everything they do for the Church, the
institution, must clearly be in the service of the Church, the people
of God. They must decrease in order that the living Body may
increase. The going gets sticky here, I know, but I can give an
immediate "for instance." On Refreshment Sunday, the Bishop of
Rome distributed bread to the poor. Did that act exalt the Church,
the institution, or the Church, the People? Were they empowered to
be themselves the feeders of the hungry, the clothers of the naked,
the freers of the captives? Or did it make misery for the moment
more bearable? And when clergy march on picket lines, as clergy,
does that empower lay people, or does it relieve lay people of their
necessity to confront the powers and principalities? Once when I
talked like this, a priest told me he felt I was putting him on the
shelf. If he really meant that—that he felt the real action was in the
world, maybe his vocation is to the lay ministry. This is not to suggest that the institutionally ordained have no responsibility for the
world. As members of the laos, the people of God, they have as
much responsibility as the non-institutionally ordained; but they
belong there AS LAY PERSONS. The priest in the Parent-Teacher
Association or in the political caucus takes his/her signals from the
ministers called to, ordained for that area: the educators, the parents, the ward leaders. In fact when the People of God are functioning in those secular areas with wisdom and love, the priest knows
that his/her ministry in the Church, the institution, has been to the
glory of God.

A Biblical Base for Ministry

by Verna J. Dozier

I have a way of mulling over things in my mind, and sometimes seemingly disparate pieces—or at least, pieces developed at disparate times—fall together.

Sometime ago I sent a memo to my colleagues at The Alban Institute, asking how we judged if what we did was worthwhile. I thought we were clear about what we were doing, and I thought we would say we were doing it well. But the question I wanted to raise was "Was it worth doing?"

I think the only way that question can be answered is in terms of what the Church is in business for.

The worth of any ecclesiastical activity, it seems to me, can only be judged on the basis of whether or not it enables the church to be about its business.

What is the Church's business?

I posed that question to an interdenominational group of clergy, and I said what I thought it was not.

Not soul saving. God has already done that, and nothing can be added to God's almighty work.

Not legislating morality. That's shifting sand and lures us away from the Biblical call to repent.

Not social service. The need for the church to do social service is eloquent testimony, to me, that we have failed in our business.

So what is our business?

Ministry.

I have been in the business of talking about the ministry of the laity long enough to know that that word hardly conjures up what I read as its Biblical meaning.

So I designed an event to help people explore that Biblical meaning. I have used it with a group of Presbyterian leaders, clerical and lay; a parish group; and two larger denominational groups, all with clerical and lay participation.

It can be done in six hours and combines time for private reflection, Bible study, and sharing.

Design

FIRST HOUR

1. Have participants in silence respond to three questions, written on newsprint one at a time:

What is your definition of ministry?

By that definition, what do you do that you consider ministry?

What difference does your ministry make in the world?

2. Have participants seek out someone they do not know so well or at all and share what they have written and listen to what the other has written.

3. In the full group ask participants to tell what they heard that was new or exciting to them.

Break

NEXT TWO HOURS

1. Have someone read aloud, while others follow in their Bibles, Luke's report of Jesus' first sermon in his hometown: Luke 4:16-21.

2. Ask the participants to reflect in silence on these questions:

What was Jesus' definition of ministry?

What did he set himself to do by that definition?

What difference did it make in the world?

3. Ask participants to share with a new partner.

4. In the full group ask them to report on what they heard.

5. Do Bible study on the passage:

a. Have it read in the various translations available.

b. Solicit questions and answers about the meaning of the words, the setting, the event, the place in the Gospel, the connection with the Old Testament.

c. Complete the passage, Luke 4:22-30.

d. Note the difficulty the radical demands of ministry can get you into.

Lunch break

ONE AND A HALF HOURS

Conflicting Images of Ministry: Mark 10:35-45

a. Have the passage read aloud.

b. For silent reflection, pose the question: What of James and John in there in you?

c. Share with someone you feel close to.

d. Bible study on the passage.

Break

ONE AND A HALF HOURS

Scope of and Empowerment for Ministry: 2 Corinthians 5:12-20a

a. Have the passage read aloud

b. For silent reflection, pose the question, What ideas come to your mind around the notion of ministry as ambassadorship for Christ?

c. Sharing in full group

d. Bible study

Concluding comments on the day.

Many participants found the day troubling. All had their ideas of ministry stretched.

Ministry, discipleship, diakonia is serious business.

To know what we are about, I think we have to ponder that Biblical message.

New Challenges for the Institution

Jacqueline McMakin with Rhoda Nary has been developing a process by which the institutional church can take seriously the ministry of the laity.

Emma Lou Benignus offers ideas about the ministry of older members of society.

David Young, in his teaching and writing on the ministry of the laity, has developed a process for equipping the saints through supervision. The process was envisioned for lay workers in a church setting, but can be applied in equipping for ministry in whatever context ministry is performed.

Empowering the Ministries of the Laity: How Congregations Can Go about It

by Jacqueline McMakin and Rhoda Nary

Ask laity who are deeply motivated and strongly committed to ministry how they got that way. You get a variety of explanations:

—"A certain book turned me on."

—"People I know have been strong role models."

—"A retreat experience opened my eyes."

—"Participation in small groups made me take a deeper look."

The influence of the local congregation is often not mentioned, or is at the bottom of the list, or is even seen as a hindrance to helping laity understand and implement their calling to ministry. Yet empowering laity to claim their ministries should be a chief task of the congregation. Are there ways it can do this job more effectively?

This question was put to us as trainers by Ed White, the Prebytery Executive of the National Capitol Presbytery. He wanted to gather a pilot group of pastors, offer them training in empowering their own and others' ministries, and also generate discussion among them about how congregations can be more effective in this important task.

The skills training that we offered is a course called "Discover Your Ministry and Gifts" (published as one of four courses in *Doorways to Christian Growth* by Harper and Row). It helps participants address six questions:

1. What are my unique, God-given gifts?
2. How can I be a patron of another's gifts?
3. Which piece of God's vision is mine?
4. What is God calling me to do?
5. Is there a corporate dimension for my vocation?

6. How do my unique gifts and calling tie into the larger body of believers?

From the experience of facilitating this course over twelve years, we knew it to be effective in raising people's consciousness that they are called by God to minister. It also gives tools they can use during the course as well as in an on-going way to discern more specifically the nature of that call, the vision that motivates it, and the gifts that implement it as well as how others can be involved. We knew that as people address these questions seriously, their lives can be changed.

"We know these courses can be effective with individuals," said Ed. "But what about churches?" Or more specifically, what kinds of attitudes, programs, and emphases must a congregation have to support the process of discerning and developing the ministries of all its people?

To tackle this question, we first described four ways of perceiving lay ministry. One way to see it is "work in the church" which is done, not simply as a job but as a result of sensing a call by God. Another perception is that it is "discipleship in the marketplace," work done consciously in partnership with God. "My whole life is ministry" is another way to look at it. And finally, ministry is seen as "faithfulness to God's specific call wherever that may be."

In struggling to portray graphically these four ways of seeing lay ministry, we came up with a diamond:

How We See Lay Ministry

"service in all of life"

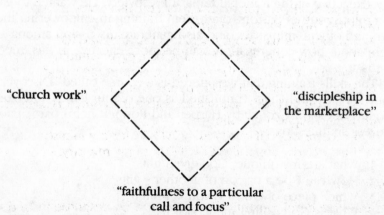

"church work"   **"discipleship in the marketplace"**

"faithfulness to a particular call and focus"

Recognizing that there are many understandings of the term "lay ministry" and a correspondingly great variety of ways to describe it, we felt that these four descriptors were graphic enough in portraying four distinctive perceptions.

"Church work" ministries are commonly the ones most recognized and supported by local congregations. Advocates of "marketplace" ministries point out that most laity have jobs outside the church and urge that more attention be given to the understanding of these jobs as ministry. Then there are people who say, "My ministry is everything I do for God's glory every day of the week—car pooling, work, family life, recreation, community activity—all of it is ministry." Others emphasize attentiveness to God's call and focusing on that in the church, in the world, in all of life—wherever God calls.

The diamond shape for our lay ministry diagram seems fortunate in that it reminds us of baseball and the importance of covering all the bases. All these perceptions of lay ministry are valuable and need to inform and challenge one another in each person's life.

The question then becomes how can local congregations support these understandings of ministry as they are lived by their members?

Toward the end of our seminar, Ed White prepared the following paper for our consideration:

Enabling Lay Ministry

As a member of the church I am most likely to fulfill God's purpose in my life if:

1. My consciousness is raised to realize that ALL CHRISTIANS ARE CALLED TO MINISTRY.
2. I am led to discover my GIFTS and to discern my CALL.
3. I find SUPPORT for my ministry and also a way to be ACCOUNTABLE for my ministry.
4. I am intentional about my SPIRITUAL FORMATION.
5. The LANGUAGE AND THE LITURGY of the church affirm and support the ministry of the people of God in the world.
6. My ministry is VALIDATED by the church.
7. The STRUCTURES and ROLES within the church recognize, affirm and support my ministry.
8. I receive CONTINUING EDUCATION for my ministry.
9. I gain clarity about the CONTENT of my ministry.

Questions:

If these nine developments are essential to my response to God's CALL, what resistances might I expect to find to each of these developments . . .

in myself?

in my pastor?

How can these resistances be overcome?

What would a congregation look like if these nine concerns were shaping its life?

What would be the role of the pastor?

Using this paper as stimulation, participants came up with the following ideas which can be used by congregations who want to support the ministries of their members.

Worship/Liturgy   This is the time when there are the most people present at church. There are a great many ways ministries can be empowered during worship. Prayers can be offered for the ministries of people in the congregation. A good example of a general way to do this is the "Litany for Those Who Work" in the Presbyterian *Worshipbook*. This includes prayers "for those who buy and sell," "for those who entertain us," "for those who keep house," etc.

In most congregations there are times when special recognition is included for those engaged in certain "church work" ministries such as church school teachers. Similar kinds of recognition can be given to "marketplace" or other types of ministry as well. For example, one pastor whose church was planning such recognition for church teachers included a blessing and recognition for all those within the congregation whose profession is teaching.

Sermons or homilies can include examples and stories of various kinds of ministering people. Those congregations which have "moments of mission," times during worship when one of the congregation's ministries are described and recognized, can also include descriptions of ministries of the "marketplace" or "all of life" variety such as corporate management, military service, peaceful protest, caring for children.

Most churches celebrate special days during worship. Mother's and Father's Days and saints' days are common. What about Law Day to celebrate ministries of people in law or using Labor Day to bless the vocations of all in the congregation? One church we know invites parishioners to place symbols of their work on the altar. Farm tools, kitchen utensils, and office log books send a strong messsage that all kinds of work are valued by God.

These are just a few of the many ways lay ministry in its variety of understandings can be empowered by liturgy.

Training/Formation   A common shortcoming of congregational training or formation programs is that they are piecemeal or fragmented. Research has revealed that people hunger for movement in the spiritual life as well as increased ability or skill in ministry. "Why do we feel we are still in spiritual kindergarten even after we have attended innumerable adult education offerings?"

The lay academy approach to training and formation addresses these concerns for spiritual deepening. This refers to a training/formation effort that is ongoing, that incorporates increased challenge and movement in its offerings, and that provides core experiences for training in discipleship plus elective offerings to teach ministry skills. The four courses in our book constitute a suggested curriculum for the core offerings in an academy. There are other suggested designs in print. Using existing designs is a way to get started in launching this kind of integrated approach to training/formation. Eventually, however, leaders trained in using these methods in congregations may want to design and offer their own courses in the basics of faith.

Training and formation in congregations can be designed to resource people at different points in their pilgrimage and can incorporate cognitive as well as experiential approaches. There can be lectures, well chosen books and pamphlets that inform, as well as small groups where people can develop and practice being community to one another.

It is worth noting that the pieces of training most often missing in congregations are ministry discernment and ministry skills training. No wonder people do not feel empowered in ministry. There are few opportunities to examine the whole concept of ministry in depth, to discern one's own calling, and then to receive some training in that calling. In *Christianity and Real Life* (Augsburg), William Diehl describes the kinds of skill training needed to prepare for various ministries.

When a congregation takes the lay academy approach to training and formation, it sends a powerful message about what it considers to be basic training in the life of faith, even though during one period of time it may be able to offer only one piece of that training.

Much more can be said about training/formation. A look at how any profession prepares its members (to be a dentist, for example, requires training in theory and skills plus a period of apprenticeship) can ignite a more serious and comprehensive approach to training in the congregation. It has been said that churches commonly give serious attention to education for membership but tend to neglect training for ministry. Most congregations have the talent and gifts among members to do both well.

Work with Individuals   No amount of group training can substitute for work which must be done individually at the point of ministry discernment and development. Most congregations have some way of supporting individuals in crisis. Widespread clinical pastoral educational programs equip pastors to offer psychological support and sensitive referrals. What is often neglected is the support of people who are not in crisis—the many people in fairly stable situations who yearn to make their lives count, to contribute meaningfully to society, to do their part in embodying Gospel values.

These people may need only a little time and attention. A conversation about vocation or an invitation to consider spiritual direction—these are ways to help people become more fully aware of God's call.

Language is important. People who are comfortable with theological language complain sometimes that others are not interested in faith matters or don't think in terms of "call." We have found many people interested in the subject of vocation, rewarding work, or contributing to peace and justice, but they may not couch these yearnings in theological language. "What are you doing with your life?" is a question of great importance to a wide variety of people. The church has unique resources to offer, but must be prepared to meet people where they are, speak language they understand, and work with people individually as well as in groups.

Retreat/Sabbatical   Sensitive writers on the spiritual life refer to the necessity of balancing sabbath and ministry time. James Fenhagen in *Ministry and Solitude* (Seabury) insists that intentional periods of disengagement are absolutely necessary to empower disciplined engagement in ministry.

This has radical implications for congregational planning. With burnout and fragmentation key problems for church people, every planned activity must be submitted to a litmus test, "Will this refresh our people or contribute to depletion?"

Congregations reported to be effective in empowering ministries build in times of retreat, disengagement, and sabbatical for people as an important part of their spiritual care. The retreats they make available are not simply for official board members but for all. They are not for working or planning but are times when work is laid aside and participants can place themselves before God to experience more fully God's compassionate love and justice and choose more deeply to be God's person in every aspect of life. That means generous amounts of silence, for being, not doing, not simply two hours of silence in the midst of a working weekend.

The whole sabbatical concept also means honoring people's need to say "no" as well as "yes" to ministry opportunities within or beyond the congregation.

Ministering Communities   For ministry to flourish, an ongoing diet of spiritual nourishment and the support of caring people are key ingredients. More and more people want to combine these elements in one commitment. They are tired of participating in task forces for ministry, prayer groups for nurturing connection with God, and community gatherings to get to know people. These important aspects of Christian life—prayer, community, and ministry—can be combined in one group. When they are, this group can rightfully be called a ministering community.

Three types of ministering communities can flourish in any one congregation and fit different people's needs. One kind is the "committee turned into community." This happens when a liturgy committee, for example, decides to incorporate spiritual development activities and personal support of one another as vital components in addition to its task of planning worship. Group theory describes the importance of people knowing and caring about each other as well as receiving inspiration for their common task both together and alone. These activities, far from being a waste of time, are vital to the mission of the group.

People whose primary sense of ministry is related to work in the "marketplace" often find "ministry support groups" helpful. In these, each member may be in a different work or ministry situation and come together for prayer, caring, and support. Sometimes these groups meet on the job, for example, in a factory or a company. Or in a congregation all those in the field of health care may gather for support in this ministry.

A third ministering community is what can be called a "mission group." This means that all of the group members feel called and want to join in a ministry together. In a given congregation, there might be mission groups devoted to a variety of concerns such as low income housing, to enlivening the prayer life of the congregation, to ministry with the bereaved.

An unfortunate development in some churches occurs when someone gets the idea that "what this congregation needs are neighborhood groups . . . or ministry support groups . . . or . . . ." and mistakenly thinks that one kind of group will fit everyone. Ministry empowerment is better served when congregations have a variety of small group options available to members.

Communication   Church newsletters and bulletins are another part of congregational life where ministries can be supported. How important to include material on all the understandings of ministry we have described! Stories of ministry projects or particular individuals, recognition of extraordinary and ordinary faithfulness or accomplishment in ministry, descriptions of ministry opportunities, small consciousness raising pieces on theology of ministry —all can have a place and send a message that ministries in the church, in the world, in all of life, and as a response to call are blessed and supported.

Budget/Resources   What message do congregational boards send to laity when there is a line item of $500 for continuing education for clergy (and there is one clergy person in the congregation) and $500 for continuing education for laity (and there are 600 laity!) What conclusions can be drawn about a congregation that will give $1000 a year to a person attending seminary with the intention of being ordained and cannot offer $100 for a member to attend a hospice convention? What about the congregation that annually sends 10 church school teachers to a religious education conference but cannot find the money to establish a job finding club for unemployed members?

These are tough questions. But they reveal what is commonly known—that congregations usually offer financial support primarily and often exclusively to "church work" ministry support. Experience shows, however, that when congregations offer financial help to support all the ministries we have described, much comes back to them in vitality and committed participation. A common worry is, "If we give to one, won't we have to give to all? So maybe we'd better give to none." It doesn't seem to follow that if one receives, all will ask. Churches can set up guidelines for processing requests. To turn them down as a policy, however, sows seeds of disappointment that may have long term negative effects.

These, then, are some of the ways congregations can empower all the ministries of their people. These ideas have been tried and work well. None is unusual. What is unusual and very much needed is for each congregation to look at all aspects of its life and incorporate the kinds of suggestions described here in combination with one another. In that way, it can strengthen the climate of support, provide the structures, and offer the training that effective long term ministry commitments require.

Jacqueline McMakin and Rhoda Nary are partners in Doorways, a collaborative effort to think anew about lay training and church structure, 4820 N. 27th Place, Arlington, Virginia 22207.

Challenge to Ministry:
Opportunities for Older Persons

by Emma Lou Benignus

These thoughts concerning older adults, their roles and responsible participation in society, are addressed to the churches. Therefore, we turn to our Jewish-Christian heritage for an understanding of the possible, rather than only to secular data and theories of aging. Let the reader be warned: We shall explore the questions that arise with a bias we proudly own.

It is to be hoped that in the decade of the eighties the churches' concept of ministry of the laos (the whole people of God) will:

Recognize that the most elderly, as well as the young, are potential channels of God's grace;

Realize that spiritual gifts and the fruit of the Spirit are given by the Holy Spirit to old people, too, for their fulfillment and for their use in ministry;

Be supportive of old people's yearnings to relate and to contribute;

Be aware that a person can be born anew at any age.

When asked what they wish, rather than what they need, many older persons say, "To make a contribution," "To let the remaining years count," and even "To help my family by dying well." A woman of eighty-five who had just heard a prognosis of her imminent death turned from her doctor to her priest to say, "Being dead and gone doesn't bother me, but what I do want is to make it clear to people that life lived here with God is every bit worth living all the way through. I don't want to contradict that in any way. If I begin to garble that message, will you help me keep it straight?"

Note that this old woman:

Realizes her way of living and dying can convey a message about God;

Is quite clear about the statement she wants her life to make, that *with God* life is good;

Knows she might, in spite of her intentions, betray the best she knows;

Looks to her fellow Christian to help keep her faithful.

To have a mission, a purpose, a contribution to make and "promises to keep," and to want to come through to the last of one's days with integrity are the activity of the Spirit within. The physical limitations of aging may actually enhance this inner life. "Physical decline may limit productivity, but the activity of the Spirit continues through shifting the central focus of personal identity from doing-in-the world to being-in-the-world, from what one does to who one is. As physical activity diminishes, the movement of the Spirit is toward an emphasis upon the nonphysical aspects of life. We all know individuals who in the face of seemingly overwhelming physical disintegration still face life with vitality that clearly is not based in their physical well-being. This vitality is evidence of their Spirit at work. It is plainly recognizable in the later years of life."[1]

To fail to engage this Spirit or carelessly to deny a person's capacity to serve is to consign that individual to loneliness and close down a life before its natural time. The experience of an aged man comes to mind. Early one morning he was found peeling potatoes and humming to himself in the kitchen of the "home" in which he lived. Curtly reprimanded for his intrusion and punished by being confined to his room for the rest of the day, he muttered, "A man's got to be a man to live." Here it was: the yen to "be up and at it," the desire to do something of value, the longing to take part in life as others do. Do we nurture these values in childhood only to quell them in old age? We need to understand that, deprived of significant living, many die spiritually before their physical death.

A kind of loving interplay with all that is is one of the Spirit's gifts to older people. Out of their own pain and longing comes a heightened sensitivity to the needs of others. When society diminishes these persons' self-esteem by viewing them only as recipients with nothing to contribute, it takes away hope and meaning. We might ascribe such error to social ignorance of human nature. But when the church of Jesus Christ, who gave his life for others and calls us to do likewise, persistently supports only ministry *to* rather than also ministry *by* the elderly, it compounds society's sin.

The year 1935 marked the beginning of Social Security and the arbitrary designation of sixty-five as the age for mandatory retirement. It was expected that retirement with a modicum of assured income would give opportunity for the freedom to pursue one's choices. It was not expected that retirement would carry social opprobrium, or the message, "You're through now, someone else is replacing you. Forget all this and have a good time . . . somewhere else." Many negatives were suddenly linked with the sixty-fifth year. American society, including the churches, has on the whole accepted this negation of human resourcefulness with dehumanizing indifference.

It is unfortunate, to say the least, when the local church does nothing at the time of a parishioner's retirement to remind that person that every member of the body of Christ by virtue of Holy Baptism is drawn into the company of the Spirit, the church, and that every member therein is endowed with charisms, gifts of grace, and significant spiritual capacities to be used for the good of all.[2] "To each is given the manifestation of the Spirit for the common good" (1 Cor. 12:7). If churches were to take seriously the apostle Paul's assurance of spiritual gifts, and if it became established practice for congregations to help their members identify, use, and enjoy these gifts, no Christian would need to fear that the years ahead will have to be uninvolved and meaningless.

The church's role is to awaken each of us to our giftedness. With Paul, it must say, "I remind you to rekindle the gift of God that is within you" (2 Tim. 1:6). To each man and woman of whatever age, the caring friends in the congregation might say, "Find out who you really are, for you are made in the *image of God*. Discern how God has been present in your life all these years. How does God call you now to be friend and servant, relating with Jesus Christ to the world God loves?" The privileged role of Christian friends in the congregation is to support the retiree, to recognize that "God did not give a spirit of timidity but a spirit of power and love and self-control." In such circumstances, with fellow Christians we can find the courage to take on our share of both joy and suffering for the sake of the Gospel of God who "called us with a holy calling, not in virtue of our works but in virtue of his own purpose and the grace which he gave us in Christ Jesus ages ago" (2 Tim. 1:7,9).

With such reminders stirring them to action, a group of older church women became active in the civil rights movement in the 1960s. They gathered momentum and supporters as they moved through the communities. Their dignity and informed declarations on behalf of civil rights and justice for all citizens gave others the courage to speak out, too. Several found themselves in jail, two of them wives of retired bishops and one the mother of a state governor. In a newspaper interview they expressed the wonder they found in being older and being free to witness to the values and conditions they hoped would prevail throughout the country, not only for the sake of the deprived but also for the sake of their own grandchildren and their children, that all might be free to become the persons God endows them to be.

These women gave classic expression through their civil rights ministry to the mark of maturity identified by psychologist Erik Erikson in his well-known account of human development, *Childhood and Society*. As people move through their years they come into different stages of concern and openness. Those psychologically more mature tend to develop concern for the welfare of oncoming generations, as opposed to a primary fascination with their own good. Erikson's term for this capacity is "generativity," the gift of caring about the good of those yet to come. Another capacity that marks maturity as reported by Erikson is the desire for personal integrity, for life to be authentic, for coherence between professed values and life as actually lived. This yearning comes through in common parlance as a desire to set the record straight, to be accountable for one's life. When passions such as these dominate our later years, it is not surprising that the heart and conscience of many older people are opened afresh to the Christian gospel. Well-springs of love and commitment deeper than ever before can be known in these years—and usually go untended.

As one reads the Hebrew and Christian Testaments, it is easy to gain the impression that when God wanted to bring about a significant change in the world, old people were called to the fore. Abraham and Sarah, both in their nineties, were the channels through whom God began a lineage of Israelites. When Israel was captive in Egypt, Moses and his brother Aaron, already in their sixties, were summoned to lead and console the people in their forty years of wandering in the desert. When something utterly new was about to break upon the world, the elderly Elizabeth and Zechariah were entrusted with the birth and rearing of John who became the Baptist, heralder of his cousin Jesus.

The older man Joseph was given to Mary as husband, ostensibly to protect her in a situation too daunting for youth. After the angel's annunciation to young Mary, she "went in haste" to spend three months with Elizabeth and Zechariah, one assumes in order to steady herself in faith through the company and wisdom of this older couple. When the infant Jesus was presented in the temple, it was old Simeon, staving off death, who first recognized him as the awaited Messiah and who warned Mary that her heart would be pierced by her son's suffering (Luke 2:34-35). And then the very old prophetess Anna, long cloistered in the Temple, when she saw Jesus "gave thanks to God" and went out to speak of him to all who were looking for the redemption of Jerusalem. Not only were these older persons vehicles of divine action, but they spoke prophetically through canticles and hymns that have become part of the treasured liturgy of the Western church: Zechariah's Benedictus (Luke 1:78–79), Simeon's Nunc Dimittis (Luke 2:29–32).

John Koenig, professor at Union Theological Seminary, wrote in his sensitive essay *The Older Person's Worth in the Eyes of God* that in Luke's gospel

> New things happen to older people.... (They) receive a vital ministry to perform for Israel, precisely in their last days. In fact, it is only in old age that they come to experience their true vocation....

> In Luke's treatment of older people we do not find the conventional expectation encountered in most cultures ... that the aged are primarily bearers and guardians of ancient wisdom. No, according to Luke, God chooses old people as bearers and proclaimers of the New Creation. They are visionaries, futurists, people charismatically gifted with a clearer picture of God's unfolding plan than their younger brothers and sisters.

Koenig finds in Paul's New Testament letters similar presentation of elderly persons as trailblazers and adventurers in God's creation. Paul himself was sixty when he planned his new and most extensive ministry in Spain (Romans 15:22–29). Summing up his findings about old and young in Scripture, John Koenig gives these comments:

> The young see visions, they are intoxicated by novelty. Age helps them to distinguish between true and false novelty ... a pseudoradicalism which actually wants to cut itself off from all roots. For Luke, older persons exercise a prophetic ministry which enables young people to see the "big picture" of God's plan for salvation....

> In spite of losses and physical disability degeneration is not the core of reality. For Christians, the really real is transformation, a daily re-sensitizing of ourselves to the ... goodness of God out of which new ministries by older persons can emerge. No one is too old to experience a blossoming of charismatic gifts for

ministry. No one's life is too far gone to become a place for the Spirit's empowering self-disclosure[3]

Opportunities for ministry change with the changing times and circumstances of the older person. The old cliche about "where there's a will, there's a way" is often proved valid. What God makes of our offering, however small, is God's business, as is illustrated in Mark 12:43–44. A poor widow gave two small coins, and Jesus said to his disciples, "This poor widow has put in more than all those who are contributing to the treasury. For they all contributed out of their abundance; but she out of her poverty has put in everything she had." As we give to others all that we have left to give—a hand wave, a smile, a look of gratitude, a word of praise—and offer it in Jesus' name, we take part in ministry. A woman on the edge of blindness, with very little left of a once abundant life, begins her day by standing at her window where all she sees is a bit of light and praises God for the gift of life. "It is wonderful so to enjoy God's riches," she says. Her daily prayers of praise and the love she radiates pervade the home where she resides.

The book *I Can Still Pray*[4] speaks of the spiritual capacities of the elderly. It is a tribute to a woman whose body has been deteriorating for twenty-one years. Now, after yet another stroke, she was physically helpless. When a visitor began to commiserate, she countered optimistically, "But I can still pray." In circumstances of extreme limitation she found purpose for her life and reminded her visitor that she retained the most basic of functions for a God-related, faith-filled life—the capacity to pray!

Because he believed in the reality of spiritual power, a young minister wanted as much of it as possible circulating in the congregation. So he invited the six housebound members of the church to form a prayer team with him. Every Sunday the morning service is taped and delivered, along with copies of the intercession list, to each team member. Although separated, the team has a corporate prayer time every morning when the priest is saying the daily office. Throughout the rest of the day they offer prayers for people on the intercession list or hold them before God in meditation. The priest and team meet weekly by means of a telephone conference, and he spends an hour with each of them every six weeks to discuss their own spiritual development. Currently, one of the men on the team is helping a recent convert learn to pray. One of the women has a small prayer and Bible study group that meets regularly in her home.

How superb it is when the seasoned members of the congregation take new clergy and their spouses under a welcoming wing, to retell the story of the parish's history, distinguish between its sacred traditions and its sacred cows, alert them to areas of sensitivity, and befriend them with the trust, hope, and candor that can grow in the aging years. Most important of all, there could be prayers daily for the new leaders, that they be faithful and a conduit of blessing for all.

Five years ago the Episcopal church introduced *Age in Action* in the church schools. Each teacher was urged to invite an older person or two to share a class session, giving young and old a chance to interact. In some churches this has become an avenue of continuing intergenerational contact in a setting where the norm separates the ages for learning. In class, children and elderly can pray together and discuss that about which they pray. In imagination they can relive Bible stories, envisioning themselves as companions of Jesus, and then talk about the experience. With activities of this sort, the Scriptures and the faith journey become meeting ground for the generations. Those who for years have served the altar and cared for its adornments can teach the young.

For older adults who come to church, an occasional opportunity for a leadership role is important not only for them but for the rest of the congregation as well. A lay reader who could no longer climb steps read the lesson from his pew with the aid of a microphone. A long-retired rector, still dear to the congregation, was invited back for homecoming Sunday. Now in a wheelchair, he preached from the center aisle. Practical solutions to difficult situations can always be found, if the desire is there.

A widow, desperate with pain over her husband's sudden death when they were both seventy, continued to "pray a psalm a day" as they had done all their married life. But now she also read the psalm aloud to transcribe it on tape. When the tape was filled she gave it and a small recorder to a widowed blind man all but lost in grief not unlike hers. Her reaching out to him was the beginning of his return to sociability and later to the church.

The losses of later life cannot be escaped, but they can be transcended to become occasions of spiritual growth as we learn to incorporate them into ministry on behalf of others. In a profound sort of way, ministry is not really an option; it is an essential expression of the nature of our being, an avenue of our fulfillment, our response to being made in the image and likeness of God.

In God's amazing way with us, when needs arise the answer is usually already there somewhere, "waiting in the bush" as was the ram when God asked Abraham to give up Isaac. There is a great need today for the loving care of young children, as mounting economic pressures send more mothers to work and as single-parent families proliferate. The incidence of child abuse increases steadily. Where is the answer? In part it may lie in matching these patterns with another social phenomenon—the largest number of available grandparents and great-grandparents in good health our society has ever seen. We need each other.

In Eastern and Southern cultures, as well as in traditional Black society, the grandparenting role is assumed as a dependable component of the family's life. Our housing patterns and industrial mobility, plus our affluence, have separated the generations in this country. Thus there is a great opportunity for many older men and women to lend a hand to working parents and their children as surrogate grandparents. A new form of three-generational ministry, called Family Friends, has been launched by the National Council on the Aging in Washington, DC. Volunteers are in homes one to three times a week to be with young children, or the chronically ill, or disabled, to relieve the family caregivers. Participants in this program can be reimbursed for expenses, travel, and meals, so that none who are willing need to be deprived of the opportunity to give of themselves.[5]

There is more value and carryover influence than meets the eye in this kind of relationship. From a survey of professional colleagues, the author of this article discovered that, when seeking inspiration and value, the memory turns to a grandparent or grandparent surrogate more frequently than to any other significant person. Psychological studies show that bonding between the first and third generation tends to be smoother, more endorsing, and more enduring. The suggestion has been made that if generations seek to live together, the first and third might do better than the first and second.

The ministry of hospitality was lauded in Jesus' day. Can the senior members of our society restore it? Last summer the Church of the Brethren made travel for families easier by staking out a trail across the country of Brethren households available for bed and breakfast. Many of the host homes were those of older adults with rooms to spare and time to be hospitable. A program for family members visiting hospitalized patients was started by the hospital's Pink Ladies team (mostly older adults) who knew peers nearby with houses now shorn of family of their own. Owners who were willing to become hosts and hostesses were given guidance for opening their home to paying guests. They also received training in responding to persons in bereavement.

The need for voluntary service in our society is as wide as the imagination can conceive. The Shepherd Center in Kansas City, Missouri, is a Methodist program that matches the skills of senior volunteers with needs in the community. In England, where cash flow is generally much less than here, the parishes have instituted Barter Societies. An older man will dig the garden in exchange for some of the landlady's canned produce after the crop is harvested. A crippled woman will care for two small children in exchange for their mother doing her shopping and laundry. Once a month everyone involved in the Barter Society goes to church and stays for a small meal with the rest of the folks.

In the United States our approximation of the Barter Society is the Self-Help Group Movement. About 3,000 self-help groups now exist, with members helping one another by providing friendly support, understanding, skills, practical information, and the kind of consolation and encouragement that can be given by someone who "has been there." These groups recognize that everybody needs support systems and that systems we had long counted on are now eroding due to changes in society, new family patterns, legislation, and various factors beyond our control. These "talk-it-over" and "lend-a-hand" groups are voluntary. They meet in churches, community centers, homes, sometimes with a professional invited to provide special training. But for the most part, members help one another, as friends do, by drawing on their own accumulated resourcefulness.[6]

The role of teacher's helper in some public schools attracts older volunteers. Their stories are sometimes poignant. A lonely, widowed retiree responded to the school's SOS for helpers. He was assigned to a class whose teacher suggested, "Come and just be around, take it as it happens." One day a withdrawn eight-year-old girl attached herself to him, saying nothing but staying close. Eventually, in bits and pieces, she told her story of sexual abuse, physical neglect, and isolation in her own home. Thanks to this quietly listening grandfather, the child was rescued. Another child, a hyperactive boy who when left alone could not concentrate enough to learn, found a friend in an older volunteer who sat with him and calmly, patiently talked with him. In this aura of quiet, loving, daily attention the boy could do his work and learn.

Older volunteers have the gifts of time and love to share. From them the emotionally disturbed, affection-starved, acting-out children who can turn a classroom into turmoil may receive the attentive care they need—care that cannot be bought.

Concern for the quality of education is prominent in the conversation of a church retirement community on the West Coast. An eighty-four-year-old said, "Let's not just talk about it, let's do something about it!" There now exists a "writing alliance" between a group of retirees interested in writing and an equal number of young people from a nearby school. They meet regularly to share their work and critique it. Comradery, mutual respect, and self-esteem are nurtured in this intergenerational venture. In addition, the art of writing, grossly neglected today, gets good support. We underscore this experience as an excellent illustration of how a value recognized as important by the senior generation can be activated in the young when the two generations experience it together.

Many older adults find gratification and meaning in reaching out to others in a wondrous variety of services and supportive enterprises. Others, in numbers gradually increasing, are involving themselves in issues and situations where political, social, institutional, or legal change is necessary to assure justice and peace at home and abroad and to further the public good. Older people with discretionary time are sitting in on city council and school board meetings, and in sessions of environmental protection agencies and public-health boards, to check chicanery or to further much needed two-way communication between such agencies and the general public. Still others organize for public attention and change.

Two retired men, one concerned about what is happening to our trees and the other a skilled fisherman concerned about polluted water causing cancerous fish, spoke of their interests with several Boy Scout troops from whose membership a nucleus of Young Citizens Concerned has been formed. This is "generativity" at work in the best of ways, young and old together caring about God's world.

Many religious groups and individuals concerned about public affairs, ecology, health, and other issues find that the adult courses developed by the American Association of Retired Persons are excellent resources available at no cost, ready for leaders in churches, local libraries, and clubs to use. A retired high school principal responded to one of these, the 55-Alive driver training program designed to help senior citizens be safe drivers. He corralled twenty-five retired colleagues from church and school contacts to set up the course in four Illinois counties. Now it has spread throughout the state and met with such success that the Illinois state legislature presently assured a 10 percent reduction in insurance premiums to those who pass the course. The 55-Alive program was conceived by older people, for older people, and is taught by them. The Illinois law was passed as a result of lobbying by older citizens. Older adults in action to save lives!

Twenty-six denominations maintain a Washington, DC, office for government relations, with some of their work done by volunteer legislative assistants. Older adults apply for these positions, which provide excellent training in legislative and political processes, valuable preparation for a leadership role back home where voting counts. The elderly have a larger percentage of voters than any other age group. In addition to the voting box, there is always the mailbox, an implement increasingly used for today's participation in sociopolitical change. Human justice and world survival issues merit much more attention than they usually receive in the churches. Where are the elderly as active agents in creating a better future? Is this their role? We affirm it is uniquely their role. Their disestablishment is a gift, an opportunity to dream of a new order, to pursue visions of new structures and ways of functioning as well as new alliances to replace the tightening knots of injustice and self-concern, discrimination, and greed.

As they emerge from cocoons of dependency and self-doubt, the aging begin to become themselves—persons with strong instincts for the good of coming generations, with compassion for humanity deepened by their own losses and suffering through the years. They are clear about the futility of relying on material and physical realities for dependable security or salvation, and they are old enough to have experienced through repeated wars the madness of the military approach to world peace. We have among us many models of the integrity, the courage, and the faithful selflessness of Spirit-led older persons. They come from all cultures and every economic level. Let us form the most heterogeneous groupings we can, to learn to hear each other, to discover the contributions each can make to further the freedom and well-being of all people. Who and what can stop older adults? Nothing except their own lethargy. God has given to generous numbers the privilege of surviving—a gift to be used for the larger creation, not just in self-interest.

By the year 2020 there will be forty million people over sixty in the United States and nearly six hundred million in the world. If we exist at all by then, mobilization for a new world order will be under way *by negotiation*. We believe "that the new world order can be promoted by older people, the group most free to do it.[7] If the ministry of older people can become *prophetic* as well as existential, older members then can serve the world as the Spirit's instruments of social transformation.

As surely as God gives gifts to the elderly, the elderly are intended to give gifts of themselves to the world.

It is the role of the churches to nurture the ministries of their members, whatever their age.

NOTES

1. "Spirituality During Aging" by Ernest G. Hall, Epping, NH (unpublished paper presented at the 36th Annual Scientific Meeting of the Gerontological Society of America, San Francisco, 1983).

2. *Discover Your Gifts*, Workbook, Christian Reformed House Missions, Grand Rapids, MI 49560, 1983.

3. *The Older Person's Worth: A Theological Perspective*, Presbyterian Senior Services, New York, NY, 1980. (Symposium at Union Theological Seminary)

4. *I Can Still Pray*, C. W. Peckham and A. B. Peckham, Otterbein Home, Lebanon, OH 1979. (Out of print.)

5. Write Family Friends, Project Director, 600 Maryland Ave., SW, Washington, DC 20024.

6. Write New Jersey Self-Help Clearinghouse Nationwide, Saint Clare's Hospital, Denville, NJ 07834.

7. "Aging and World Order," Jim Baines, *The Whole Earth Papers*, No. 13, Global Education Association, 552 Park Avenue, East Orange, NJ 07017.

Equipping the Saints through Supervision

by David S. Young

A method or supervision is needed which can concretely help persons grow in their ministry as well as grow in maturity in faith. With the above concept of leadership we can see that such a manner of supervision is not that of one person telling another what to do. Rather a method needs to be employed wherein the one doing supervision affirms the unique talents and gifts of another in ministry. The servant leader does this by centering on the growing areas of another and seeing how a process for supervision can aid another to come into fullness of his or her ministry.

In order to accomplish this, a contract is formed whereby a person is supervised in ministry. In such a contract an equipper delineates a relationship with another person to provide very specific helps. The contract outlines what persons are expected to do, for how long, and in what manner assessment will occur. All this is done with the fundamental understanding that such a process will lead to a dynamic growth in faith as one claims a ministry and works through the growing pains of implementing a calling.

The Supervising

Supervision is the overall program in which the equipper works with the one being equipped to develop a fullness in ministry. Supervision is drawing forth talents and skills of individuals so that they can make gains at their growing edges. Rather than giving all the answers or telling persons how to act, the equipper trusts that people are children of God and that this process of supervision will help them discover God's purpose in their ministry. Increased awareness of God's activity should result from being supervised. In fact, spiritual guidance is one of the chief functions of the supervisor.

Supervision builds a trust relationship in which the roles of supervisor and supervisee are clearly defined for the purpose of doing ministry. The supervisor helps a person implement a plan by acting as observer and helper. The equipper does accept a role of authority. More than just a passive observer, the supervisor offers definite help and guidance within the boundaries of the integrity of the relationship and the autonomy of the supervisee. Supervision means active reception, sensitive responses, specific approaches, and long term investment. Seven stages of supervision suggest themselves.

Listening

One of the best ways to begin supervision is to listen. In a first session, the equipper may sit down with another person and simply say, "Tell me about your ministry." Unless someone is very reticent, the words begin to flow. The level may vary according to the trust prevailing. However, if a contract has been formed, persons are usually willing to talk about their ministry at some level. Just to have someone listen may be an entirely new experience.

Several things happen in listening. Listening has a way of affirming another in ministry. It conveys that this ministry is important. Someone wants to hear about it! Such feelings can be conveyed in a multitude of ways in supervision, and they are very confirming to the person in ministry. The fact that someone else takes this ministry seriously, underlining strengths as well as embarking on a period of growth, tends to strengthen the individual. Confirmation through listening becomes a stepping stone for growth.

Just as a mirror highlights new aspects of already familiar areas, so listening enables persons to make new observations for themselves about their own experience. In fact, listening begins the process of attentiveness to what one is doing and to what God is doing. Quietness, receptiveness, and searching are established. Listening can lead one into exploring new areas that were heretofore undiscovered. Listening begins to raise intentionality and focus on what may have become routine and stressful. Growth begins.

Supervision starts with attentive listening. The equipper listens with one's whole being. The equipper notes nuances of meanings, body language, and faith expressions that come through. The supervisor may repeat in similar language what is being heard so as to demonstrate that a person is understood. Such paraphrasing also serves in a way that the supervisor can build upon the conversation. Certainly in supervision, it can be most helpful to comment as well as to mirror. "You really have been teaching an interesting class."

"The youth ministry has had some high moments and some low moments." "I am impressed with the sincerity and the devotion with which you have been working." All such comments may be appropriate.

Conversations are done in a confidential manner so that the individual feels heard but not overheard. Such confidentiality sets a pattern for growth and conveys that growth is in the offing. A person is at this point today. Tomorrow can be different. In fact, if times have been exasperating, the equipper may have something to do with changing the situation. Support and encouragement can often be rendered through listening. Listening lays the important groundwork for all that is to follow in supervision.

Identifying Growth Areas

A second area of work for the supervisor is to create support around primary issues. The supervisor does this by supporting the ministry of another in general. By listening, by encouraging, the supervisor helps a person identify where growth may occur. A topic keeps re-emerging. A question is posed. A dilemma is present. The equipper works to help the person identify these areas. The supervisor may ask the person what is meant in a certain area. Identifying, clarifying, and summarizing are all important functions of the equipper.

The one doing supervision resists the temptation to offer advice at this moment. It could be easy to tell persons what they could do differently. That time may come as trust builds. However, a person's walls of resistance can go up or a person can feel like giving up if there is a sense of someone better quickly pointing out one's failures. Instant advice can shortcut the process. It can also set up the dynamic of expert and novice whereby the newcomer always runs to the equipper for advice. In fact, ownership can be built for the one being equipped if the equipper explores where the individual wishes to grow and keeps the initiative in the hands of the one being equipped.

At this point it must be recognized what role the equipper takes. The equipper needs to do adequate homework by studying and conferring on the area of ministry in which supervision is given. Rather than providing all the answers, the equipper becomes knowledgeable in the issues and resources which are at hand. In this way growth is not skewed to personal issues of either equipper or the one being equipped. Supervision is a combination of information and interaction. A sense of training pervades because the equipper is seeking to be a facilitator into the wider arena of ministry for the one being supervised.

The overriding perspective in identifying areas for growth is to establish the approach of coming from strengths. From that vantage we can lean into weaknesses. The equipper may say that achievement has come in one area and now growth can follow in another. Without belaboring the point, the skill in building positive confidence will have a dramatic effect on the success of the ministry being performed. Supervision is not dissecting people to find their weaknesses. Rather it is enlarging their base of understanding and helping them move into more creative and responsive ministry.

Asking Permission

An important third step follows directly behind listening and identifying areas for growth. This is the step of asking permission. "Would you like to work in this area?" the supervisor asks. The one to be equipped has made a contract and in general has asked for help. Now the offer of help becomes more specific. Permission is asked in order to focus energies and to seek consensus. Perhaps the one to be equipped says, "No, I'm not sure that this is the exact issue." Together the equipper and the equippee work out the area for growth in a mutual identification. This is supervision at its best.

Asking permission is a step not to be overlooked. It shows respect. It ensures that a person is not being violated. It communicates that the other person is in control. Asking permission in fact lifts up the person. If the one being equipped takes responsibility for growth, then learning becomes a permanent style. What a gift for ministry! Ministry that is faithful to Christ has growth as its hallmark.

Asking permission and receiving consent frees the supervisor to go to work. Rather than trying to squeeze in a thought or word of direction, now the supervisor intentionally explores areas of growth with the individual. There may be areas at first which the supervisor might need to hold back in exploring out of respect for the confines of the agreement. However, as confidence develops in one area, the way often opens to even harder areas. Asking permission opens the process that leads on with time and growth.

The "yes" of response, when it comes, is a confirmation that supervision has been happening. Proper staging has been done. Listening has been effective. Timing has paid off. The yes is an invitation to come in deeper to the process. One yes leads to another. Initiative is built for the person to discover new growth areas. The evaluation process therefore becomes a welcomed part of the contract. Yes indicates receptivity, initiative, and response. It even leads the equipper into greater intentionality in the work of supervision. The yes indeed is ultimately a yes to God's initiative which is leading all along the way in growth in ministry.

Discussing Resources

A fourth step is discussing resources about ministry. Discovering resources becomes the responsibility of the one being equipped. Very quickly as one growing in ministry begins to search in the resources, new leads emerge. Names arise in articles; pieces are suggested in footnotes; workshops are advertised. While discovering proper resources takes time and energy, it is an important skill to learn for growth in ministry. Unhelpful books and articles need to be weeded out. A perspective is being developed. While energy is expended to discover new and creative resources, the effort will pay great dividends in formation for ministry.

The time comes for the equipper to discuss these resources with the one being equipped in order to draw benefit from them. The question may be raised, "What are you discovering about your ministry in your reading?" "What did you find in terms of the growth areas in which you are working?" These kinds of questions draw us back to the objectives of the contract and the goals of the ministry. The purpose has included learning about ministry in general but also in one's area in particular. Equipping is an educational process.

Resources can provide that objective third voice which can be helpful.

Developing Action Plan

The fifth area of supervision is to help an individual develop a plan of action. A person may share with the equipper what plans have been emerging. The supervisor will listen and help discern what patterns have been developing in ministry. Then the equipper can help clarify the directions being considered and help one look ahead at results of each possible course of action. The equipper may also observe the comfort with which the one being equipped feels with each option. Helpful feedback is not only in order but in most cases is expected by the one being equipped.

Also at this time, it is good for the equipper to raise topics around the identified growth areas. For example, the equipper may observe that a similar pattern could develop here which developed for the person in the past. The person in ministry may be totally unaware of the fact that the situation in which one finds oneself has similar dynamics to former experiences. If delegating has been a struggle, the reminder by the equipper to delegate may be very appropriate. Also if progress is being observed in a person's goals then the supervisor can underline such growth with positive feedback.

As new avenues are explored in a ministry, the supervisor may suggest other alternatives. New options may be utilized; new ideas can be injected. Without becoming overbearing or recalling endless tales, the equipper may add, "In my experience I have found that this works but that that usually has limited effect." Or the equipper may say, "What would happen if you concentrated in this area and de-emphasized that focus?" The supervisor can serve as a real resource, highlighting options and anticipating probable consequences. Growth is set in the context of action.

Supervision calls for the best of planning. Often the supervisor can help the supervisee break down the steps toward a goal. Establishing time lines, intermediate steps and proper interventions can be helpful. The equipper helps the one being equipped to continually evaluate what is happening with a ministry. The discussion can range from discussing how things are going to how an event matched hoped-for objectives in ministry. What was achieved? What was learned? How can we alleviate any shortcomings? How did one grow in ministry?

Supervision can take on the form of helping a person in ministry sort out the new steps to take.

Supervision enables a person to develop a plan of action. The supervisor becomes the needed helper to work out a course of action. Also the one equipping helps a person keep check on the growth areas for ministry. In some ways the equipper helps the person growing in ministry to be able to hold it all together. While not rescuing a ministry when all is seemingly going wrong, the equipper is there to help the person over the rough spots. The supervision can help the ministry gain a momentum which ensures progress and growth.

Modeling

The sixth area of supervising is modeling. An equipper does not say, of course, that one is going to sit down and model what the

equipped should become for others. However, this is in fact what
one does and the more one is aware of it the more intentionally it
can be done. The one being equipped certainly needs to learn to
listen, to support another individual, to help identify growth areas,
to set up and facilitate a program, to learn about themselves, others
and God. The equipper does provide a pattern which has application for ministry.

Modeling is important because the equipper is an example of
the merger of belief and practice. What one is becomes just as
important as what one does. If the one being equipped believes in
the authenticity of the equipper, then the process will be a powerful influence in one's formation in ministry. In fact, religious formation in general may be at its height in training for ministry. Modeling is therefore a self conscious aspect of the equipper's work.

The topic may emerge directly as to what ministry means as the
one being equipped asks why the supervisor is acting in a particular
manner. Doubts may be raised. Questions may be asked. The equipper must be prepared to identify with the struggles in ministry and
explore how these are handled. This dialogue can be invaluable.
The equipper can explain the reasoning behind suggestions and
actions. Questions raised in supervision can be very helpful for the
supervisor. All concerns are openings to share in the nature, calling,
and purpose of ministry.

The best preparation for the role of modeling is to keep growing in one's own ministry as an equipper. The equipper sets the
pace. The equipper will be handling the frustrations, ambiguities,
and tough decisions which come with ministry. By handling these
in a constructive manner, the equipper signals that ministry is an
intentional vocation. The equipper keeps stretching and growing.
The practitioner in ministry is the teacher of ministry. Renewal of
one's ministry through this whole process becomes merged with
being spiritually alive, the seventh topic of supervision to which we
now turn.

Spiritual Awareness

The equipper has the willingness and readiness to lift up the spiritual dynamics as they arise and relate to particular areas. Theology is
the thinking about God in concrete situations of life. The equipper
is attempting to relate in a way that maintains a total awareness of
the person of Christ. All along the way we become aware of what
Christ's kingdom is becoming. Spiritual awareness should therefore

not be an add-on but rather an integral part of each area and avenue of supervision.

Therefore development of the spiritual life of the equipper is key. Only a life rooted in deep prayer will have the awareness needed for supervision in ministry. Continual opening to the Living Presence is the resource which will yield the creative urges needed in supervision. A regular discipline of Bible study will result in a Biblical awareness that is constantly informing the supervision process. Spiritual awareness results in a peace which enhances the very relationship the equipper has with the one being equipped. Keeping alert spiritually will keep the equipper attuned to spiritual needs of the one being equipped as well as of those served in the ministry at hand.

The equipper therefore demonstrates values which are being implemented in ministry. How one responds to emergencies or unusual situations becomes very important in the teaching role which supervision takes. What has been done has laid the base. Now we face how to practice in ministry what we proposed when we did not necessarily set up the conditions. The authenticity of ministry comes as one uses one's beliefs to respond as Christ's presence. If the style of the servant leader shows through then the spiritual awareness is being turned into a real ministry as equipper.

The Alban Institute:
an invitation to membership

The Alban Institute, begun in 1974, believes that the congregation is essential to the task of equipping the people of God to minister in the church and the world. A multi-denominational membership organization, the Institute provides on-site training, educational programs, consulting, research, and publishing for hundreds of churches across the country.

The Alban Institute invites you to be a member of this partnership of laity, clergy and executives—a partnership that brings together people who are raising important questions about congregational life and people who are trying new solutions, making new discoveries, finding a new way of getting clear about the task of ministry. The Institute exists to provide you with the kinds of information and resources you need to support your ministries.

Join us now and enjoy these benefits:

Publications Discounts:

☐ 15% for Individual, Contributing and Supporting Members
☐ 40% for Judiciary and Seminary Executive members

Discounts on Training and Continuing Education

Action Information, a highly respected journal published 6 times a year, to keep you up to date on current issues and trends.

Write us for more information about how to join The Alban Institute, particularly about Congregational Memberships, in which 10 designated persons (25 for Supporting Congregational Members) receive all benefits of membership.

The Alban Institute, Inc.
4125 Nebraska Avenue NW
Washington, DC 20016